Post-200

# Post-2000 Poetry of Dissent

## Comparative Readings

### For students of
### International A-Level English Literature

Abha Prakash

PETER LANG

Chennai - Berlin - Bruxelles - Lausanne - New York - Oxford

Bibliographic information published by the Deutsche Nationalbibliothek. The German National Library lists this publication in the German National Bibliography; detailed bibliographic data is available on the Internet at http://dnb.d-nb.de.

A catalogue record for this book is available from the British Library.

Library of Congress Control Number: 2024932883

Cover image: © Abha Prakash, Author's classroom, Future School, 2021.
Cover design by Peter Lang Group AG

ISBN 978-1-80374-507-7 (print)
ISBN 978-1-80374-508-4 (ePDF)
ISBN 978-1-80374-509-1 (ePub)
DOI 10.3726/b21876

© 2024 Peter Lang Group AG, Lausanne
Published by Peter Lang Pvt Ltd, Chennai
info@peterlang.com – www.peterlang.com

This publication has been peer reviewed.

*To my late father*
*Dr Ishwar Prakash Gupta*
*For letting me choose the directions of my life*

# Contents

# Preface

The need to create an interpretive guide to the post-2000 selections of poetry included in the Edexcel IAL English Literature syllabus came into being in the context of several factors. I had taught the twenty-eight poems of the new course since 2016 to four consecutive batches of highly motivated English Literature learners from diverse racial backgrounds that included Indian, Korean, Swedish, French, German, Spanish, Dutch, Russian, and Italian. For most students who had grown up in Auroville, English was their second language although, in general, their language fluency stood at a good level when they entered the A-level segment of high school.

Secondly, given the level of difficulty many students encountered while studying the prescribed poems by British and Irish authors in the *Poems of the Decade* anthology, I realized that there existed a real need for an accessible, easy to understand collection of critical essays for the hundreds of students who sit for the International A-Level English Literature exam each year in India and other Asian countries and who approach the contemporary poetry section with some trepidation. This resource tool would benefit not only students in my own classroom but also the many others whom I could never meet.

The third, and perhaps most crucial contributing factor behind this book was the general lack of critical material in print. While other sections of the syllabus such as Shakespearean drama, pre-1900 poetry, and even mid-twentieth century drama had sufficient and in-depth literary criticism available, there was a paucity of reading strategies within the post-2000 poetry section. Online forums such as Intrepreture.org, and A-level Revision Blog were in existence, the latter a commendable peer effort by UK students themselves, but there were not many platforms offering contextual guidance to understanding the poems in a comparative mode.

Analyzing post-2000 British poetry is not an easy task and writing a meaningful critical essay of 700 words in an hour's time is even more daunting. The fact that over four years several of my students secured high rankings in the subject exam proved that international students had the capability to do well and enjoy studying the Pearson Edexcel course as much as I enjoyed teaching it.

Abha Prakash
September, 2023

# Acknowledgements

This book took shape in the aftermath of the biggest crisis in my life.

In May 2022, I opted for voluntary early retirement after teaching English Literature for around nineteen years at Future School, Auroville, an international town in south India. Following my last class around May 21st, my students and I went for ice creams at a local restaurant. Ten days later just as I was sending out book proposals to publishing houses, I fractured my ankle on both sides.

Following surgery, I found my right calf and foot in a cast and a long, non-load bearing recovery period ahead of me. In the five or six months that I became house-bound, I divided my energies between physiotherapy sessions, my part-time editing job, and writing the introduction and fifteen chapters contained in this book.

I am grateful to my publishing editors at Peter Lang, India, and the UK, for their enthusiasm, patience, and constructive feedback on the manuscript. To all my professors at the Department of English, Hindu College, University of Delhi, Delhi, and the University of Saskatchewan, Saskatoon, Canada, a warm thanks for their encouragement and continued goodwill. I wish to also thank my PhD supervisor, the late Professor Carol Morrell, under whose insightful guidance I wrote my doctoral dissertation in the 1990s.

Thanks are due to my mother, Dr Sudha Prakash, for being a pillar of support despite her own health problems. To my husband, Agni, for taking over some responsibilities of our teenage children, especially buying the groceries and making the evening meal until I was able to get around. To our domestic help, Lakshmi, for shouldering added burdens.

To my sons – Aditya and Akshay – for being a source of joy and support in my life.

I love you.

# Abbreviations

A few long titles have been shortened in the chapter discussions to abbreviated forms for the sake of convenience. Shortened titles (given in parenthesis) have been used for the following poems:

1. "A Leisure Centre is also a Temple of Learning" ("A Leisure Centre")

2. "The Furthest Distances I've Travelled" to ("The Furthest Distances")

3. "The Fox in the National Museum of Wales" to ("The Fox")

4. "From the Journal of a Disappointed Man" to ("From the Journal")

5. "Look We Have Coming to Dover!" to ("Coming to Dover!")

6. "Fantasia on a Theme of James Wright" to ("Fantasia on a Theme")

# Introduction

Many contemporary poets from around the world today are letting go of rigid conventions of form and structure, preferring to create more fluid modes of presentation for their verse. The new millennium poetry can be characterized by its irregular form and structure where stanzas are uneven in length and sometimes absent altogether. Poems of today can easily be mistaken for prose, as several poets use a simple, colloquial lexis rather than rhymes and metre. Although a few poets continue to use classical moulds to present their poems, poetry in the current milieu continues to flourish in new and unusual forms. This is not to say that only contemporary poetry is *avant garde*. Almost all waves of new poets in every generation over the past 800 years and maybe even earlier, have in their own way subverted previous trends of expression.

Reading different authors from varying time periods helps to make this clear. In British poetry, for example, we can find consecutive waves of poetic movements introducing newer modes of presentation and thought, different from its predecessors. As literature cannot be produced in a vacuum, historical, social, personal, and cultural conditions invariably influence the writing process. The Middle English period produced Geoffery Chaucer (1342–1400), the father of English poetry, whose early writings were influenced by the French text *Roman de la Rose* (circa 1250) as well as the medieval social, religious, and economic realities of his time. His masterpiece, *The Canterbury Tales* (circa 1392), with its witty and ironic insights into the imperfections of human nature remains a popular text that is widely studied in literature classes at university level all over the world. Similarly, the later Renaissance not only produced the love sonnets of Shakespeare but also the clever metaphysical poetry of John Donne and Andrew Marvell characterized by its unconventional scientific conceits and logical arguments. The two legs of a compass, for example, could be used to describe the steadfastness of a long-distance love relationship. And a man could seduce his coy mistress to enter sexual union using far-fetched metaphors and analogies despite the strict moral codes of the seventeenth century. Similarly, the early nineteenth century saw the emergence of the nature-loving Romantics who were deeply influenced by the idealism and passion of the French Revolution, and who were in turn succeeded by the more pragmatic Victorians who preferred to deviate from the spontaneous expressions of their predecessors. Radical views of a fragmented world emerged in early twentieth century poems that were influenced by Modernist trends of the 1920s and these in turn shifted to the unsettling deconstructive modes of the post-war years where personal identity could not escape the mark of the political.

It is true to say that every age of poetry has dissented, broken away from the literary conventions of the past, thinking of itself as the harbinger of change – with new forms and new voices of expression. Contemporary poetry is no different.

## Post-2000 Poetry of Dissent

One can argue that most of modern literature can be characterized as the literature of dissent in some form or other. The two world wars, rising literacy levels across race, gender, and class lines, along with the freedom struggles of the colonized in Asia and Africa led to the dissolution of the imperialist empires in the mid-twentieth century and the birth of a new self-awareness. The parallel acceleration of feminist movements and post-colonial writings in the 1960s and the 1970s contributed to a unique literature of the dispossessed that has continued into the twenty-first century. These emerging voices are heterogeneous and an effective counter to the dominant literary viewpoints coming from more privileged backgrounds.

The idea that poetry is written in an ivory tower, far removed from reality and the struggles of life has long disappeared. While the writer needs to be plugged into the imaginative realm while creating a poem, the world necessarily enters a writer's fictional text in some way.

In the many years that I have taught literature in its several genres at secondary and post-secondary levels, I found myself asking new batches of students the basic question of whether they thought literature had a role to play in society. In fact, why did they choose to study literature? Could reading poetry and prose widen one's awareness about the world? Could fiction rise above escapism and speak the truth? Could dynamics of power be hidden in poetic narratives, in assonant verse and symbolic imagery?

These questions drew us deeper into a discussion of art versus reality. Does art have to imitate reality or should art transcend the mundane and reinvent uniquely subjective, well-crafted windows to the world? In the end the either-or debate does not win. The literature of any country gives the reader glimpses into its cultural and social diversity, where the writers' choices regarding the aesthetics of form and structure are their own, and where the freedom of a writer's personal expression counts above everything else. This is especially true for poets as they literally have the right to exercise what is known as *poetic license*. It is also important to note that contemporary poetry is challenging the very notions of what makes a poem "literary" or "not literary."

********

While our scope in this book is limited to a discussion of the twenty-eight poems and poets[1] from *Poems of the Decade (2011)*, an anthology prescribed for students of the UK Edexcel International A-Level course, I will give a brief overview of what sets apart this poetry in general and what shape dissent takes in these poems. In my view a text that challenges conventions in any form or degree is a disruptive text. This questioning of established norms or world views can take place on the level of language, literary features, structure, point of view, theme, and voice. A text that speaks from the margins, gives a voice to the voiceless, makes deliberate use of dialects and non-standard English, and breaks away from classical moulds and narratives can be considered subversive and political.

Out of the twenty-eight poems discussed here, only a few are shaped in specific poetic genres. Sinead Morrissey and Sue Boyle have adopted the villanelle, a poem of nineteen lines. But because the villanelle typically

---

[1] The poets included in the A-level syllabus were born between the 1920s and the 1970s. Many of them are still writing today.

uses rhyme, only Morrissey's "Genetics" comes close to the original form. Similarly, Tim Turnbull's "Ode on a Grayson Perry Urn," imitates the ode form used by John Keats (1795–1821) in his ten-line stanzas, but the modern poet parodies the form and content of the nineteenth century poem "Ode on a Grecian Urn" (1819). An ode is traditionally a poem of praise, but in Turnbull's hands it becomes a satire. Some poems like John Burnsides' "History" reinforce meaning through its distinctive spacing and line formatting, while others like Adam Thorpe's "On Her Blindness" use the traditional two-line stanza that cannot technically be called a couplet as it lacks metre and rhyme. This lack, however, does not diminish the poem's power.

The selected poems are each stylistically unique but some commonalities can be traced. One of the prominent characteristics is the use of prosaic language and a deliberate turn towards colloquial expression as in Helen Dunmore's "To My Nine-Year-Old-Self" and Ian Duhig's "The Lammas Hireling." While some critics may see this as a loss of literary merit, others may perceive it as a way of rejecting the established norms by which poetry has been judged so far. Another feature that can be identified is the use of one-line and one-word stanzas, or even one-word lines. Examples can be seen in "The Gun," "Out of the Bag," and "The Deliverers" as well as "A Leisure Centre." The one-line stanza, when placed in a poem containing longer stanzas, plays the role of a climactic statement, something that jolts the reader into paying more attention to the text.

There are poems that follow no specific rules of structure, literary or otherwise. John Burnsides' "History" contains frequent half lines that give a fragmented visual image to his poem. There are also lines that contain only a single word. Ciaran O'Driscoll's "Please Hold" is a polyphonic poem that uses deliberate dissonance and a confusing structure to convey the chaotic misadventures and frustrations resulting from automated communication in our technology-dependent modern world. The poet takes a commonplace situation and transforms it into an effective comment on our systemic dependence on artificial intelligence. Consequently, the poem is a strong reaction against the seemingly harmless established order that demands compliance and conformity in the name of progress.

George Szirtes' "Song," an inherently musical poem with a simple, rhyming lexis, is a subversive text which recalls the fight against oppression within the context of the anti-apartheid movement. It echoes the songs of resistance that evolved among the enslaved peoples in different parts of the world and celebrates a single woman's efforts to unite the oppressed through non-violent methods and thus bring about empowerment.

A set of poems that question war and terrorism and speak for the protection of our fragile planet and all living creatures are no less political. Man-made weapons and even garden tools like the chain saw are capable of mindless destruction if put in the wrong hands. Poets like Simon Armitage, Vicki Feaver, Ciaran Carson, Ian Duhig, and Roderick Ford speak of the dangers of violence and its impact on our individual and collective psychological health. Although the form and structure of these poems seem traditional, the poets' distinctive use of voice, tone and language are modulated to create subversive content.

There are poems that speak from a personal space and yet raise important questions about women's rights. We can study Patience Agbabi's "Eat Me" and Tishani Doshi's "The Deliverers" as profound attacks on patriarchy. Poets such as Ros Barber, Eavan Boland, and Sue Boyle question the feminine conditioning of the girl child based on their narrators' own childhood experiences. Every female poet included in the selection reveals a mindset that strongly rejects traditional or conservative ideologies.

Intertextuality is another feature that can be found in a few of the poems where a canonical literary text is referred to in a direct or less direct way. Turnbull's "Ode on a Greyson Perry Urn" has already been discussed above. Daljit Nagra's "Look, We Have Coming to Dover!" is another example that draws the reader's attention to Victorian poet Mathew Arnold's "Dover Beach." Like Turnbull, Nagra subverts the older poem to focus on his own political agenda. He specifically emphasizes the hardships suffered by Third-World immigrants in Britain. It is quite apparent that Nagra challenges Arnold's poem on the level of theme as well as on the level of language. He deliberately uses English in ungrammatical ways to show how power dynamics exist among people who use standard forms of language to marginalize those who lack fluency, in this case, the immigrants. The intertextual reference to Mathew Arnold's "Dover Beach" is ironic because

Nagra's description of the beach and the "scummed" cliffs of Dover is far from complimentary. Nagra's poem, despite its scathing attack on Britain's insensitive treatment of its immigrants is, however, more optimistic than Arnold's melancholic poem with its underlying pessimism and loss of faith.

Another instance of intertextuality, albeit non-textual, occurs in Sean O'Brien's "Fantasia on a Theme of James Wright," which attempts to follow the stylistic modes used by the Deep Image Poet James Wright. It makes a pointed reference to a specific painting called "*Going Home*" (1888) by the nineteenth century artist Ralph Hedley who raised awareness on the plight of miners through his art. Like Hedley, O'Brien chooses to focus on the underprivileged lives of the miners who face hazardous work conditions and who sacrifice their lives underground while the world above is unaware of their struggle.

Poets like O'Brien, Nagra, and Doshi, who choose to write about human rights are poets of dissent. In fact, the voice of questioning the status quo emerges as a consistent feature in many poems of this selection.

While writing this book, someone asked why I decided to title it *Post-2000 Poetry of Dissent* when most poems were, according to the person, written for a mainstream audience and by privileged British poets such as Simon Armitage, John Burnside, Sue Boyle, Carol Ann Duffy, and Alan Jenkins. The person had obviously not read the selected poems.

Even though three of the above poets were conferred the title of Britain's Poet Laureate,[2] does that make *all* their poetry popular and mainstream? We can perhaps concur with Susannah Herbert, Executive Director of Forward Arts Foundation, when she asks readers to "treat this anthology with caution. It looks harmless but contains multitudes, works that speak of violence, danger and fear alongside love and longing, in forms broken and reshaped by the need to communicate what it is to be alive now, here." (Preface, *Poems of the Decade*)[3]

---

2    Carol Ann Duffy was the first woman Poet Laureate of Britain from 2009 to 2019. She identifies herself as a "poet and mother" but does not mind being regarded as a lesbian role model. Currently, Simon Armitage is the Poet Laureate until his term ends in 2029. His poetry is versatile and cannot be limited by the "mainstream" tag.

3    <https://www.theguardian.com/books/2015/mar/16/poems-of-the-decade-anthology-forward-prizes>

One of the aims of educators and curriculum developers especially at the secondary level is to help students discover a range of knowledge and diversity of viewpoints within each discipline. The case of English Literature is no different. With hundreds of new novels and poetry collections being published each year, how does one select what is worthy of being studied in the high schools of today?

The Pearson Edexcel IAL English Literature specification (2015) includes an independent component on post-2000 poetry at the AS level. Students are asked to study around 28 poems that were published in Britain and Ireland between 2000 and 2010.[4] This anthology, *Poems of the Decade: Forward Book of Poetry (Forward Worldwide, 2011)* contains recent award-winning or shortlisted poems by poets still writing today. The fact that the anthology includes male and female writers from diverse races and cultural origins, a variety of poetic styles and subject matter, and includes canonical as well as lesser-known poets, makes it an extremely rewarding experience for a teacher like me who specializes in women's fiction and post-colonial literatures. Having taught this course for the last six years to four groups of enthusiastic A level students from mainly non-UK backgrounds, I found that the in-class poetry readings, and interactive analytical discussions were appreciated by students and led to their greater awareness about texts and contexts. Some of the students went on to choose English Literature at university – a fact that makes my role and contribution as a teacher well worth it.

Abha Prakash
21 September 2023

---

4    Around eight poems were removed from the syllabus during the pandemic exam series.

# A Note on This Book

Readers who use this resource guide will need to read the poems separately from the prescribed anthology. Due to copyright restrictions, I have included only minimal quotes, mostly words and phrases, for the sake of illustrating my ideas and arguments.

Students are requested to use their own discretion when choosing the second poem for writing their comparative essays in the context of the topic given by their teacher or in the Unit One exam. Please note that a poem may be compared to several other poems depending on the topic. In the essays contained in this book, I have chosen two poems that connect on a respective topic.

A glossary of literary terms and concepts is given at the end of the book for those who may need it.

The language in the following essays has been modified to suit the level of 11th grade students between the ages of 15–16, who may be preparing for the AS exam.

# CHAPTER I

# Objectification of Women in "A Leisure Centre is also a Temple of Learning" and "Eat Me"[1]

Sue Boyle and Patience Agbabi focus on similar aspects of women's lives where standards of physical beauty and sexual appeal are determined by men. They discuss how young women can be trapped in relationships where their inner worth may be dismissed at the cost of their physical desirability. In "A Leisure Centre is also a Temple of Learning," Boyle shows a nude young woman at a changing room in a spa or gymnasium immersed in a narcissistic skin care routine after using the pool. The poet filters this scene through the critical gaze of a group of older women who watch, perhaps with jealousy, the youthful beauty of this young girl who is making herself more supple and desirable for her lover. "Eat Me," on the other hand, focuses on a man's sexual appetite for plus size women and how he forces his already obese girlfriend to eat mountains of unhealthy food that he lures her with.

Neither poem gives any specifics about location in terms of time or culture. In "Eat Me," the unidentified couple could be found in any culture or country. By avoiding naming their characters or giving them a location-bound context, the poets may be pointing to the universal prevalence of women's objectification in patriarchal societies.

In "A Leisure Centre," the older women call themselves the "Chorus," like the commentators in ancient Greek drama. By comparing themselves to the Choric elders, the group of women may be drawing attention to their

1  Disclaimer
    Please note that a poem can be compared to another poem on different levels. In every essay in this book, I have chosen two poems that relate on a given topic. In the exam, please use your discretion when choosing the second comparative poem based on the specific question asked. Always remember that the two poems must have enough evidence to support a strong comparative discussion of the topic.

lived experience and how older women in modern societies have little value due to their lack of youthful bodies and skin. Boyle, however, also brings in an element of jealousy and judgement. The young woman, immersed in her beauty routine while rubbing moisturizer into every nook and corner of her body, is seen as self-centred and even as a "charlatan." The latter word choice is harsh but it makes the important point that young girls are conditioned by patriarchal beauty norms that pressure them to fit their bodies and outward appearances into false or fantasy driven patriarchal moulds, and to live life on a superficial level of outward appearance.

In "Eat Me," this includes putting on weight to please the lover. Agbabi presents the poem through the persona of an unnamed young woman with low esteem, a person who "did what [she] was told." The poem opens with the image of a birthday cake with three layers of icing to mark the woman's 30th. The readers assume this refers to her age but soon, given the man's fetish for oversized women we come to know that the number does not signify age but the woman's weight in stones.

"Eat Me," focuses on both, the victimization of women as well as their ability to stop abuse, once they become aware of their exploitation. In "A Leisure Centre," however, the older women's point of view serves as a lesson that the young can learn from. Boyle's poem critiques how women are treated in a patriarchal society, where a young woman's body can hold the key to power over a man. But this power lasts only until her youth lasts, as the older female observers testify at the end of the poem.

Both poems convey suggestive as well as overt sexual imagery detailing the physical attraction between a man and a woman. In "A Leisure Centre," the woman is described as "lithe as a young leopard" and includes an overt reference to the girl's neatly shaved "secret cleft." In "Eat Me," Agbabi details the obsessive love a man has for his overweight girlfriend and the power he exercises over her body. The references to the female body as the site of pleasure, "a jacuzzi" for the lover to swim in, is a central sexual metaphor in the poem. In both poems the female body is an object that is enjoyed and feasted upon by the male lover.

Agbabi takes this idea of feasting both ways. Given the poem's title, the poet centralizes the act of eating as a pleasurable activity. It is also the way by which the man seduces the woman in order to satisfy his own sexual appetite. By feeding the woman a high calorie diet, she becomes trapped by her "chef," in a bizarre love relationship where her extra-large body size is a necessity for the relationship to proceed further.

In the second half of the poem, Agbabi's narrator reveals her growing insecurity about her weight, her awareness of her compulsive eating disorder, her circumscribed existence, and her emotional and physical dependence on the man. In stanza six she views herself as a "tidal wave of flesh." The poet continues the woman's negative relentless, self-critical thought process in stanza seven where the phrase "too fat" is repeated four times. Due to her obesity the woman becomes trapped within the home and cannot venture in public.

With the use of the refrain – "Too fat to" at the beginning of each line, the woman judges her appearance by the harsh standards of female beauty prevalent in the world outside. Her inability to exit this relationship or to have meaningful social interactions outside her home is responsible for the building resentment against her lover, her "cook," who loves to watch her grow "like [the] forbidden fruit." Once she hits thirty-nine stones, the man pours olive oil down her throat in the hope of hastening her weight gain still further.

Agbabi's poem brings up themes of power, gender relations, domination, and victimization, and finally empowerment when the woman rolls over the man and crushes him to death. This climax gives the poem both its surprising twist and liberating ending.

The metaphor of the forbidden fruit brings the biblical reference of the fall of Adam and Eve within the revisionist context of patriarchy. In the poem, the female body is shown as an object to be tasted and relished by the male lover. Concurrently, the reference also signifies a shift in the poem from the woman without self-will to a woman with awareness of her status vis-a-vis the man. The fact that she sees her body as both an object of male desire as well as an active player of destruction creates a moment of foreshadowing that explains the ending. Perhaps it is not an accident, but a willed demonstration of her body's strength and her inner desire to be free that leads to her abuser's death.

The ending of the poem sees a role reversal – the woman as the active agent, instead of the passive receiver. "I drowned his dying sentence out" is not only an example of the poem's many alliterative instances but the woman's active intervention and control of her future. The irony of the concluding line where we come to know of the woman possibly eating the dead body of the man because there was no other food in the house serves as a strong reminder of the title, an instance of black humour, as the reader celebrates the end of the woman's torture and hopefully the beginning of her new, bolder identity.

Sue Boyle's poem, in contrast, does not offer the young woman a dramatic way out of patriarchy. In fact, the older women view her efforts at beautification with ironical poetic phrases, comparing her hand to a weaver, her hair to a waterfall. The objectification of every part of the girl's body – her breasts, her thighs, her tanned skin – all point to the fact that she has internalized patriarchal sexual norms by objectifying her own body.

In fact, this young girl with her alluring sexual body is ready to be served to patriarchy, her beauty and youth are to be enjoyed and tasted – "She is summer cream slipped over raspberries." "A bee could sip her."

The last four lines of the poem, however, show a dramatic shift – from poetic perceptions to prosaic down-to-earth reality:

We twelve are the chorus:/we know what happens next.

Sue Boyle does not give a voice to the younger woman in her poem. Is there a reason she stifles her voice? Who has the last word in this poem? Why?

Traditionally, in Greek drama, the chorus were a group of elders who commented on the play's action and who mediated between the actors and the audience. The twelve older women in Boyle's poem are on the margins watching the young girl's self-absorbed efforts to accentuate her beauty. The poem makes an important point about ageing and how patriarchal societies devalue women once they have crossed a certain age or when they have lost their good looks and flexibility.

Are the older women in Boyle's poem given a higher status than the young girl? Are they trying to protect her from a miserable future? When they say that she "should look around" what do they mean?

Both poems raise interesting points of discussion that are valuable for young adults of both sexes.

# CHAPTER 2

# Dead or Alive? Redefining History in "The Fox in the National Museum of Wales" and "History"

Robert Minhinnick's wonderfully playful poem, "The Fox in the National Museum of Wales"[1] presents history in both traditional and radical forms. While the figure of the fox is open to interpretation (is it really an animal or is it the metaphorical attributes of a fox or is it Time?), the setting the author has chosen definitively supports the concept of history as a material record of human civilization across the ages. A museum, regardless of its location, acts as a repository of artifacts or inanimate objects from the past that carry the essence of the time they represent. The radical nature of the poem can be found in the literal and metaphorical role that the fox is playing as the only living, moving being in the otherwise dead museum. His movements are tracked by an "I" figure, presumable a security guard, but the fox is too fast to be captured. John Burnside's poem that is simply called "History," challenges notions of what we deem history to be. Is it simply the time past? Does history only consist of events worth recording or is history ingrained in our present, vulnerable life forms? Both poets re-examine notions of time – of how the past and the present have the power to impact the future. The techniques the two poets adopt to present their themes are very different; both poems also differ in their register and tone. While Burnside's poem is serious and reflective, Minhinnick's poem is light and entertaining.

"History" presents two contrary ideas of Time. In the poem we can see Time as static and paralysed, disrupted by events that cause history such

---

[1] This poem was removed from the syllabus during the pandemic exam series for International A Level students.

as a war, an earthquake, or a senseless act of terrorism that kills thousands
of innocents. As soon as history is created, it becomes dead, a moment of
the past but also a moment that will be remembered for all time. On the
other hand, Time is also shown as a continuum, an ever moving, shifting
river with no beginning or end. In this scheme every moment has the right
to continue its journey, no one has the justification to order its closure.

Rated as one of the more difficult poems in the Post-2000 Poetry
course, Burnside's "History" sets its context in relation to the 911 attack
without making any direct reference to this historical event in the body
of the poem. The subtitle alerts the reader to the possible connection – *St.
Andrews: West Sands; September 2001*. The poem makes multiple references
to the beach of St. Andrews, Scotland, where the poet and his family gather
shells, and fly a kite on the day the news fills him with "muffled dread of
what may come."

Burnside begins by describing a seemingly ordinary day at the beach
while the "gasoline smell from Leuchars," a small RAF and army station, and
"people jogging" bring in allusions to the mundane world that apparently
continues despite the extraordinary event that has just shaken humanity
across national boundaries. The poem is quietly reflective, focusing on that
day when the 911 terror attack in New York made history.

The prevalent reflective mode of the poem is, however, unsettled by
the poet persona's feelings in response to the news. An uneven visual struc-
ture with irregular stanza lengths and half lines dominates the poem, per-
haps pointing to the unsteady thought process that the narrator struggles
with. The anaphoric placement of the word "Today" at the beginning of
the poem and then again ten lines later, along with the use of enjambment,
dashes, and varying, downward spacing emphasize the fragmented flow of
the speaker's pessimistic thoughts while he is trying to focus on the here
and now. It is important to note that in a poem named History, the poet
chooses to focus not on the past, not on what happened, but on the present.

In a similar manner, the first-person narrator in "The Fox" brings our
attention to the here and now using present tense to indicate the actions
of the fox who has entered the museum unnoticed and is moving through
the different exhibits and time periods at a good speed. A variety of verbs
bring out the active movements of the animal – the fox "sniffs," "skedaddles"

"shimmies," moves "between dynasties" and back and forth in time. The ability of the fox to be everywhere at the same time – the past, present, and future – gives him the quality of being Time itself. Simultaneously, the fox is an emblem of our natural world, a living force, that is perhaps trapped in the dead world of the museum.

Burnsides' narrator in "History" does not dwell on the deaths caused by 911. He focuses attention on the fragile ecosystem of the beach, gathering shells with his little son, Lucas, while trying to find the "evidence of life" in the "driftwork" around him. His reflections suggest a mix of negative and positive connotations. While collecting shells and searching for "evidence of life" point to hope, phrases such as "driftwork," "shreds of razorfish" and "tideworn" indicate a world vulnerable to destruction. In a poem that indirectly highlights the subject of humans perpetuating terror on other humans, Burnside focuses on the need to connect with nature knowing its ability to heal and regenerate. This living earth, this world, according to the poet is not something "we own." Our identity too cannot be defined "by the names" we carry, or by our social and cultural kinship. As humans, we are just that – humans. A part of this beautiful, fragile planet that we call home and that we need to protect and share with other living creatures at all costs.

In Minhinnick's poem, the museum only carries evidence of human progress or examples of humans overpowering giants of nature such as the whales. Perhaps the fox stands for the under-represented aspects of our natural world. In any case, the animal symbolizes a force of life in a monument of the past. The contrast between the past and the present is quite apparent in the poem. The narrator refers to the ages of world history – the Renaissance, the Baroque, the Industrial Revolution, the Fossils, Celtic Orthography – as well as the literary movements of Cubism and Surrealism.

The fox's swift movements, who "passes an age in a footfall" appear to be the main subject. Minhinnick's frequent repetition of the syllable "f" is not only a deliberate allusion to the fox but adds to the alliterative richness of the poem – "for at a foxtrot travels this fox" and the earlier stanza where the narrator is trying to locate the fast-moving fox – "the fox is in the flux of the foyer, the fox is in the flock." This latter reference seems to suggest that the fox cannot be seen due to the influx of the visitors who are metaphorically being referred to the "flock." This biblical reference hints at the sly and predatory attributes of the fox but there are no further references to support this claim.

In Burnsides' poem the natural world is clearly privileged over the cities and other man-made systems. The poem exhibits the very real fear of losing our world, a fear of making it history, a thing of the past, dead. The poet evokes multiple, complex symbols and images through his 73-line poem. The child, the "toddler on the beach" illustrates oneness with the environment, innocence, vulnerability, and hope. The image of the kite, at once free and rooted, uniting the earth and the sky, represents in the poem's topography the speaker's desire to be "anchored to the shore" while still "plugged into the sky." This need for humans to be grounded, to "register the tug and pull of other bodies" is a way to experience the real world despite all its contradictions, to feel empathy for and kinship with all states of life.

In the second half of the poem, Burnside makes a subtle reference to the title. He mentions the "quiet local forms of history" and then goes on to list them: "the fish lodged in the tide," the "ornamental carp … captive and bright."

While the quoted lines contain ambiguity as to the nature of similarity the poet wants to establish between two seemingly opposing categories – wild nature as opposed to animals kept in cages for human entertainment – the section makes the point that both aspects are present in our world. Why does the poet make the natural world a form of history, one may ask? Could he mean, perhaps, that the earth's natural phenomena, much older than our species, is a precious heritage that needs to be guarded and conserved?

Minhinnick seems to think so. The fox is a survivor from the past, it has evolved over the past seven million years and has survived the desert and the arctic. He deserves a place in the museum but the poet shows him avoiding capture by humans and surviving due to his stealth and skill at camouflage. The narrator claims that the fox "is something to follow … he is the future." The last lines show the human rooting for the fox's escape from the "closing iron doors" of the museum.

"History" is clearly a poem that evokes thought and reflection on life and the problematic role of humans: "how to be alive … and do no harm?"

Is it right, Burnside asks, for those who do not support activism of any sort, those of us who quietly live our lives – are we still complicit in the wrong doings perpetrated in the world?

These difficult questions are posed indirectly by Burnside. The answers will vary as we are after all students of poetry, a discipline that is at once subjective and deeply connected to the world around us.

The ending of the poem again brings together the contrasting image of the toddler on the beach perfectly in sync with the earth, oblivious to dangers, while the parents, all "nerve and line," fly the kite, "patient; afraid; but still, through everything attentive to the irredeemable."

Burnside's last phrase is emphatic about the inability of humans to save our world. This pessimism is, however, balanced by the more uplifting final image of the three humans – a father, a mother, and a child – the whole human race in microcosm, who symbolize continuity and hope.

To be human is to be connected to the fragile, the voiceless, and defenseless aspects of our world. The onward journey or evolution of humans is as important as that of the fox.

That is the only way forward.

# CHAPTER 3

# The Self and the Other in "From the Journal of a Disappointed Man" and "Ode on a Grayson Perry Urn"

Andrew Motion's first-person poem, "From the Journal of a Disappointed Man," describes a man observing a group of "macho" men constructing a pier. There is a clear division between the "I" speaker and the "they/them" group who presumably have nothing in common. The readers view them through the critical gaze of the speaker, who is a writer carrying a journal. Another poem where a group of people are put under a critical lens, judged, and mocked, is Tim Turnbull's "Ode on a Grayson Perry Urn." In this poem the speaker appears to be an older man observing a "kitschy vase" on which murals of modern youth have been painted. The urn depicts British youth in a contemporary setting of fast cars and fashionable pursuits. The poet observer mocks the vase for its unconventional design as well as the portrayal of irresponsible youth on its surface. He condemns both, the vase, and the younger generation, for falling below prevailing expectations in art and life. Since Turnbull's tone in the poem is light and entertaining, we are supposed to take his observations in a non-serious manner but that does not take away from his main theme of presenting the vase and the youth as the Other.

In both poems the "Other" is perceived as a negative, inferior force. The Self is the person who represents a group or class of people who are socially privileged in some way. The Self perceives itself as "normal," who speaks from the comfort of his or her familiar world, the world within which the Self has grown up and felt validated. The Other is anyone who is foreign to the Self, different, unfamiliar and to some extent, unacceptable within the social group of the Self. The inability to relate to the Other creates tensions, divisions and sometimes leads to conflict. In "Ode on a Grayson Perry Urn," Tim Turnbull's speaker presents the British youth as the Other. He does so not only because they belong to a generation much younger than him but because he is unable to relate to them or understand them on any level. In both poems the Other is demonized through the Self's biased point of view.

The speaker in Motion's "From the Journal," is clearly biased from the start. He does not identify himself with the construction workers although they belong to the same sex. A sense of superiority tinges his observations as we can judge from Motion's use of negative lexis. The word "paraphernalia" used to describe the workers' equipment to drive the wood pile into the water carries a hint of the dramatic. He calls the work in progress "a massive affair" and later describes the men as "massive." In stanza five, he calls the men "monsters," thus clearly developing his biased point of view.

The poem uses two parallel semantic fields, one relating to pier construction work and equipment such as "chains, pulleys, cranes" etc., and the other, more interesting one, of describing the workers as stereotypical macho men, and commenting on how they speak, move, behave etc. The latter is done with the intention to create negative images. The word "man" or "men" is repeated ten times in the space of eleven four-line stanzas.

The fact that the speaker/observer himself is a man who does not identify with these "very powerful ... silent men," who ignore him while going about their work is an important clue to understanding the poem. The poet speaker, writing in his notebook, takes on the role of judging the workers and even evaluating their strategy while the wood pile is swinging above their heads. By using a conversational style and the use of enjambment between the first and second stanza where the final lines continue into the next stanza, Motion creates a persona of a detached man, the observer, sharing his supposedly objective perspective about a group of men at work. However, a note of disrespect colours his observations in every stanza. He belittles their style of communication calling it "all monosyllables." He calls their movements "obscure" and their attitude to work as one of indifference – "for all he cared the pile could go on swinging until the crack of Doom."

Interestingly, the observations tell us more about the speaker's attitudes – his insecurities and his sense of superiority perhaps, and of course his disappointment. His mocking and stereotyping of the so-called macho men, the strong, silent males end in dismissing them as inept and passive as they are unable to finish the job and thus leave the site. The real man in the poem is perhaps the observer, the disappointed man. Even the foreman is mocked when the speaker calls him the "most original thinker" only because he is smoking "to relieve the tension."

Motion portrays the division between the Self and the Other by making the speaker appear self-righteous and normal while the other(s) are obviously the "massive" men who fail at their job. They are dehumanized and made to appear incompetent and unintelligent.

Similarly, the speaker's focus in Tim Turnbull's "Ode on a Grayson Perry Urn" is on condemning the artistic flaws of the vase, and by extension, the flawed youth painted on its surface. In the poem there is a veiled distinction made between good art and mediocre art. In the very first stanza the poet calls out the "gaudy" quality of the vase on display. Using an interrogative and casual tone, the poet hints at the vase as being less than the original, albeit imaginary, Grecian urn, immortalized by Keats in his poem, "An Ode to a Grecian Urn" (1819). By playing on a similar sounding title, Turnbull draws the attention of his readers to the nineteenth-century poem and even borrows syntactical, stylistic elements and ideas from it. Thus, a strong element of intertextuality enters Turnbull's poem which cannot be ignored.

In "Ode on a Grecian Urn," Keats, a Romantic poet, addresses it as a "Sylvan" historian, as art survives unlike the humans who create it. Keats views Art as a record of social and cultural trends as well as an object of beauty. In his poem he also includes several questions addressed to the urn. Turnbull parodies this approach by opening with some banal questions – "What's all this here?" He addresses the urn in the first stanza, after briefly describing it as "kitschy" for "delineating tales of kids in cars." He goes on to list the youth as "louts" wearing Burberry clothes, and denigrates them for causing "bedlam on the Queen's highway."[1] The readers guess that Turnbull has a problem with the rich kids living on "crap estates" just as he dislikes

---

1    An article, "Poems of the Decade anthology swaps Keats for modern masters" in *The Guardian* by Alison Flood commented on Turnbull's prize-winning poem.

modern art. The first stanza also contains the speaker's condescending and sarcastic attitude towards the urn – "your gaudy evocation can … conjure the scene" of the fast cars, their "throaty turbo roar" as well as induce a "sense of peace" in the viewer.

In terms of structure, Turnbull's poem also has five stanzas, but in contrast to Keats' poem, his words lack flow and harmony. In fact, Turnbull's sentences are full of jarring language, especially hard-sounding active verbs and include the slangy names of drugs within the semantic field of cars. The use of enjambment in stanza one and two, increases the pace and does not allow the reader the time to assimilate the accumulative details of young boys and girls speeding on the motorways. The mix of seriousness and comic satire gives Turnbull's poem an unpredictable edge where the readers are kept in a state of surprise. One instance of this is when he, like Keats, extolls the immortalizing function of art – the urn will immortalize the youth – but then makes an overstatement that they will "stay out late forever, pumped on youth and ecstasy," the latter word a pun that denotes a happiness inducing drug used among a proportion of young adults in the UK.

Turnbull's narrator uses some clever rhymes to drive his point about the youth and their fun-filled activities, including the addiction to speed, sex, and drugs. He rhymes the girls' "nervous squeals" to the "wheels" as they turn at dangerous speeds. At the same time, he borrows Keats' ideas of how art captures moments and freezes them in time. In Turnbull's satirical perspective, the cars being driven by the rash teenagers will not "skid and flip" or crash as they are just pictures on the urn and therefore removed from reality. The youth depicted on the urn are irresponsible according to the poet as they do not need to go to work the next day. They can be out all night, indulging in "crude games of chlamydia roulette" as they are rich. The reference to the sexually transmitted disease due to unprotected sex with multiple partners may have an element of realism but again the reference also reinforces the speaker's hostility towards the younger generation.

---

<https://www.theguardian.com/books/2015/mar/16/poems-of-the-decade-anthology-forward-prizes>

While the youthful lovers in Keats' poem follow conventional early nineteenth century social norms, the youth in Turnbull's poem are twenty-first century daring millennials setting new trends, showing off "their donut Os" on streets and disturbing the peace of suburban residents who cannot sleep due to the noise. The speaker makes the sarcastic remark that "tranquility" is only for the "rich."

In the final stanza, Turnbull again addresses the urn in his slangy derogatory language, calling it a "garish crock" and subverts the themes of beauty and truth that Keats used to end his famous ode with. Turnbull's parting shot is that although to him the urn lacks beauty and the youth lack direction, future generations of poets will examine the urn as a historical artifact of how "children might have lived" at a time when "truth was all negotiable."

Both Motion and Turnbull give their poems a fast-paced momentum with the use of active verbs and concrete nouns. Both poets use minimal punctuation without end stopped lines within each stanza. Motion takes this technique of enjambment further in at least two stanzas where the last line of each continues into the next stanza thus complicating the reader's understanding of the poem's meaning. Since punctuation consisting of commas, semi colons periods and dashes slow down the movement and break a poem into digestible segments, a poem using enjambment increases the momentum of the words and phrases where the reader must understand without the structural aids a poem normally uses. The poems convey a conversational style where the speaker speaks his mind with impunity. The register in both poems is more prosaic than poetic, the jarring words often conveying the irritation and disappointment of the speakers to the readers.

# CHAPTER 4

# Monster Machines in "Chainsaw versus The Pampas Grass" and "The Gun"

If a chainsaw could be given a face and a voice, what would it be like? Simon Armitage takes a common garden tool and personifies it as a cruel, blood-thirsty murderer in "Chainsaw versus Pampas Grass." Vicki Feaver's, "The Gun," a short poem composed of six stanzas in free verse, two of which are single sentences long, shows the dangers of owning a killing machine. According to Feaver, bringing a weapon into a house not only "changes it," but also damages the human who uses it. Both poets portray these two inanimate objects as having uncontrollable power in the hands of the user. While Armitage gives extremely negative human characteristics to the chainsaw while it is in action, Feaver explores the psychotic, psychological changes a gun brings to a man and his partner, the narrator, while they ready a nightmarish feast of the innocent animals they have shot.

Armitage takes personification, a frequently used poetic device, to the next level in his long poem. Composed of eight long stanzas of irregular length, the poem is written in blank verse in third-person and first-person with an arsenal of active verbs that create dissonance from the start. The narrator describes the chainsaw coming out of its winter hibernation, "unplugged," and "grinding its teeth in a plastic sleeve." This opening personification foreshadows the action that is about to come. The tool is going to be used to cut the pampas grass growing in the narrator's yard. The fact that the opening sentence and the title emphasize the "unlikely match" between the "instant rage" of the machine and the passive tall grass, again sets up the reader's expectations before the bloody fight begins. We assume it will be a one-way battle as Nature has no weapons to defend itself against human technology, and especially not against the "rush of metal lashing out at air."

In the first two stanzas, Armitage portrays the chainsaw as a human, that gulps a "quarter-pint" of engine oil before the narrator plugs the power cord, and "gun[s] the trigger." The deliberate association of the chainsaw with a gun signals the tool's fondness for killing, conveyed through the image of its "sweet tooth for the flesh of the face and the bones underneath." The chainsaw does not discriminate whether it encounters "cloth, jewellery, or hair." It has a "perfect disregard" for what is offered; it rips through anything. Interestingly, this fact points to how the chainsaw has been used by murderers to kill and dismember human victims. By bringing in the horror of human killings, Armitage deepens the frightening impact of the chainsaw on the reader's consciousness. The last three lines of stanza three are in first-person where the narrator holds up the powerful machine and feels the throb of a "hundred beats … drumming in its heart," and "the drive-wheel gargle in its throat."

In contrast to the active verbs used in describing the raging machine, the grass is presented in a more passive manner. We are told that it looks "ludicrous" with its "feathers and plumes." Despite its "twelve-foot spears" the grass is not a strong opponent. The narrator recognizes this aspect and still uses the chainsaw even though the grass could simply have been pulled out manually or "lever[ed] out" with a "pitchfork." The next few lines describe the narrator in action, using the chainsaw to destroy the poor "swooning" grass until "plant-juice spat out from the pipes and tubes."

Like Armitage's trigger-happy narrator lashing out with the chainsaw, the gun-wielding narrator in Feaver's poem feels the rush of power and control while killing "creatures that have run and flown." The setting in both poems is domestic, where the home owners seem to be normal human beings who change once these monster machines are in their hands.

Feaver emphasizes the terrible power of the gun in her opening sentence – "Bringing a gun into a house changes it." Speaking in second-person, to an invisible listener, the narrator calmly describes how an inert gun, lying on the kitchen table "like something dead" foreshadows the killings it is capable of later. The speaker, whose gender is unspecified, speaks in a slow, unhurried fashion about the sequence of events following the entry of a gun. At first one practices shooting tins in the garden and then, suddenly, the first kill happens.

Soon after this, the speaker goes on, "the fridge fills" – the alliterative phrase emphasizes the overuse of the gun. The user's hands start to "reek" of "gun oil and entrails." Again, the juxtaposition of the mundane with the image of the bloody entrails creates a shocking effect. The house floor is covered with "fur and feathers." But there is something else. Using the gun and killing animals is like an aphrodisiac, which leads to a "spring in your step; your eyes gleam like when sex was fresh."

The attraction towards using machines that can kill is a dangerous addiction. Both poems seem to show the increasing levels of masculinity and ruthlessness in the users of the chainsaw and the gun. Feaver portrays the damaged psyche of the gun user who seems to think that "a gun brings a house alive." This one-line stanza is meant to create a strong impact on the reader.

Femininity in both poems is marginalized. While the pampas grass is given a somewhat feminine fragility in the words and phrases used to describe it – "swooned," "pockets of dark, secret warmth," the narrator in "The Gun" could be a woman who reflects on the pros and cons of the gun used by her partner. In the last stanza, she decides to "join in the cooking," to make a feast for the "King of Death."

The final lines of both poems uphold the image of Nature as indestructible, at least in its plant forms. The "King of Death" is personified as "stalking" out of the forest, "his black mouth sprouting golden crocuses." The contrast of colours representing the cycle of life and death as well as the word "stalking" used to describe his style of walking appears ominous and ambivalent. Is the house now going to be occupied by Death? What do the flowers symbolize? The innocent life forms that were killed and eaten by the gun user? The identity of the narrator whom we presume is female, is problematic as well, because we are not sure on whose side she is.

The ending of "The Chainsaw versus the Pampas Grass" shows the "new shoots" of the grass springing up from the ground. By summer it is "wearing a new crown." This regeneration of Nature is a victory, and Armitage clearly shows who the winner of the "unlikely match" is, despite the destructive power of the chainsaw. The biblical reference to the "corn in Egypt" also points to Nature's powers of renewal with the chainsaw user watching the growing vegetation from the "upstairs window like the midday moon." The simile clearly conveys the defeat and eclipse of the chainsaw monster in the presence of the sunny pampas grass. Just as the moon is eclipsed in the presence of the noontime sun, so also the narrator feels defeated by the resurrection of the pampas grass.

While both the pampas grass and the chainsaw are referred to as "it," the poem brings into play their gendered personifications. To the chainsaw user and the gun wielder, killing is fun, a "game," that sparks up their ordinary lives. Armitage takes a commonplace situation of a man clearing his backyard and turns it into a merciless battle where he literally "overkills," and still gets defeated in the end. The irony of the ending is not lost upon us. Armitage continues the personification of the chainsaw until the end with the saw hanging on its hook below the stairs, "seeth[ing]" and unable to forget its "man-made dreams."

Both poets through their poems seem to convey a message against mindless and impulsive violence. If one person is capable of so much damage with the use of a lethal weapon, what would happen to our world if more people have access to killing machines?

# CHAPTER 5

# Female-centrism in "An Easy Passage" and "Inheritance"[1]

Eavan Boland's female narrator in "Inheritance" is a woman, a mother of two daughters, who has renounced the world as most of us know it. She lives in a remote, unnamed place described as an "island of waters." A life closer to nature has made her calm, self-reliant, and instinctive. The island she lives on does not appear to be populated by men. For generations women here have lived without material comforts and still managed to create a sustainable society that takes pride in its alternative way of life. A similar female-centric social fabric, albeit more conventional, consisting of a mother, her teenage daughter, and her young friend is at the centre of "An Easy Passage." The setting is urban and middle-class although Julia Copus does not specify the geographical location beyond a row of houses facing a street that contains an electroplating factory.

Written in first-person singular, Boland creates a persona who seems far removed from material desires and who has no attraction for legacies. She wonders, however, what she could leave for her daughters. The poem focuses on this very human urge – to give to one's children something precious, beautiful, that they could use or keep to remember them by. The poem celebrates the close bond between a mother and her children and the importance of sharing life's important lessons.

In contrast, Copus's third-person narrator describes a teen girl escaping her own home to join her girlfriend waiting in the driveway below. The absence of a father figure implies a single mother who is trying to protect

---

1   The poem "Inheritance" was removed from the syllabus during the pandemic exam series.

her young daughter by setting down rules. The daughter, however, views these rules as an infringement on her independence and chooses to go her own way. The fact that this act requires courage and determination makes the poem an alternative portrait of women's right to make personal life choices. We can assume the narrator is also female by her shift from "she and her" to "we," a collective first-person statement of frustration with the way women are confined as they come of age – "What can she know of the way the world admits us less and less the more we grow?" There is another female character in the poem, a secretary, who works in the office across from the house, who is watching the young bikini clad girls meet for their rendezvous outside the house.

Both "Inheritance" and "An Easy Passage" show an awareness of how the conventional world expects women to be – feminine rather than female. Gender norms shape girls and boys into masculine or feminine roles. When women reject social conditioning, however, they opt for female hood which is different from femininity. Female hood represents individuality, while femininity reflects conformity. In their own way, Boland and Copus are showing individual portraits of women who want to embrace freedom and pursue choices that are different from the roles the world expects from them.

The house, in "An Easy Passage," functions as a symbol of confinement. While feminine women regard the home as a symbol of safety and refuge, bolder women seek validation outside the sphere of domesticity.

This dichotomy between the feminine and the female woman is shown through the narrator in "Inheritance." She rejects finding anything of value that she has learned from women before her – traditional crafts and skills such as women's braiding and knitting, that result in delicate laces and shawls, all this she finds she never had a use for and cannot give to her daughters. What does this mother really want to pass on?

Using declarative statements along with enjambment to create flow from one stanza to the next, Boland's speaker uses colloquial speech patterns, almost thinking out loud in a stream of consciousness technique that fluctuates between the here and now and the past. She recognizes that she cannot offer a "view" of the mountains or the beauty after the rain. These transient moments cannot be captured except in memory. The land too, she knows, cannot be inherited by her daughters as it was never theirs to begin with.

Unlike interpretations that focus on women being denied the right to inherit property due to patriarchal norms,[2] I would argue that Boland's progressive narrator is rejecting the very idea that we can own any part of earth. Individual ownership of land is a selfish idea, that grew out of a capitalist mindset. In a collective community where there is no wealth and little hierarchy, the idea of individual ownership of land does not make sense. Enlightened beings know that no one can own planet earth, it belongs to all living creatures. It is a privilege to live on it. In contrast, the pursuit of material desires, consumerism, and possession is to undermine the very quality of being human. The poem rejects this approach altogether.

What can we surmise about this narrator? How is the poet projecting her and what kind of response is the poet expecting us to give her? Do we relate to this mother who wants her daughters to inherit useful lessons of life rather than the silver, the silk, and the crafts?

Closeness to earth and nature are qualities that Boland's narrator can be associated with, but she cannot hand over the land or the beautiful views of nature.

In contrast to the down-to-earth attitude and a simpler way of life untainted by materialism in "Inheritance," Copus in her poem, looks at life from the angle of privileged teenage girls who are half-in love with each other and oblivious to their surroundings. While the sexual orientation is not explicit, it is implied that this relationship is not acceptable to the mother. The girl's house is locked because her mother does not want her to meet her friend, or because she "does not trust her daughter with a key."

The non-poetic quality of "An Easy Passage," makes it like a prose description in a short story. The poem begins in *media res* and focuses on the young girl making the daring escape. If there are poetic elements they can be seen in the metaphors. The use of strong adjectives, concrete nouns, active verbs, and personification make the visual aspects more prominent. The "long, grey eye of the street" symbolizes the surveillance systems that women in most societies must live under. Paradoxically, the street also

2   <https://blogasenglish.wordpress.com/2016/01/13/inheritance-revision-notes/>

denotes the escape route to the outside world, away from the protected "warm flank of the house." By crafting the body of her poem into a long unbroken chunk with long sentences running into several lines, Copus creates a riveting plot of first love that cannot be separated into stanzas. Could there be other reasons why the poet chooses an unconventional format for her poem?

In the two poems, motherhood is portrayed differently. Boland's maternal narrator does not care for outward appearances, social roles, and expectations. Copus's mother figure, however, is driven by traditional ideas which seem patriarchal. The poet shapes the readers' response by not giving the mother a voice in her narrative at all. Her opinion is marginalized because she is conventional in her thoughts and repressive in her actions. Locking a teen at home and forbidding her to interact with her peers is a form of control that Copus does not support.

There is, however, a major point that both poets seem to be making, which is that women do not form homogenous communities just based on their sex. There are differences among women based on culture, economic means, and generation gap. Women can have greater understanding, the poets seem to be saying, if they understand each other's needs and perspectives but it is not easy. The irony of Copus's title is clear – it is not an easy passage to hold your own in this world, especially for younger women.

What about the secretary's thoughts in the poem? Copus's third female character, the unobtrusive observer who secretly watches the teenage girls from the interior of her cabin across the street perhaps exemplifies a person who followed social norms at the cost of her personal happiness. The girls seem lost in love, "far away from the mother ... far too, most far from the flush-faced secretary who, with her head full of the evening class she plans to take, or the trip of a lifetime ..." watches the finale of the girl "dropping gracefully" off the porch roof into the shade of the driveway below.[3]

---

3    The use of the double frame narrative, where the primary audience to a dramatic scene is present within the poem, and the readers are the secondary audience watching or reading the whole from a distance is an interesting structural tool used by Copus to deepen the visual impact. This is similar to "A Leisure Centre" and "From the Journal" poems which also contain the primary audience of one or more observers within its frame.

Is there a hint of jealousy in the secretary who is dreaming of a getaway while the younger girls have already accomplished the start of their adventure? The silver anklet around the calf of the girl and the "flash of armaments" reflecting from her shimmering toenails symbolize a mix of femininity and daring that perhaps the secretary secretly yearns for.

In contrast to "An Easy Passage," the ending of Boland's poem is understated like the rest of it. The female narrator is not making claims on behalf of other women; she is merely sharing her feelings and doubts from her own experience. Finally in answer to her own question of what she could pass on to her daughters, she remembers the night when her first child was sick with fever and how she could not sleep, but stayed watchful through the night. In the morning, when the fever was gone, she felt as if she had learned something important in a natural way, without the aid of modern medicine. Out of all the knowledge that she hopes to give to her daughters, it is this which is the most important – the innate, instinctual knowledge that lives within and around us all and which we often overlook in the pursuit of external, acquired skills and possessions.

Some can argue that the poet is promoting the feminine skill of nurturing that women have automatically ingrained in them. No evidence, however, can be found to support this claim. Boland's narrator celebrates a life of bonding within nature and promotes the need to listen to the "silence" that carries with it unspoken truths to live life by.

In conclusion both poems celebrate women, and their need to live their lives on their own terms. The omission of male voices or figures makes both these poems female-centric. On a certain level both poems are about escape from traditional societies and patriarchal expectations. The mother in "Inheritance" differentiates herself from the other women around her. The daughter in "An Easy Passage" is also different and can be seen as a rebel in the making.

# CHAPTER 6

# The Child versus the Adult Self in "Material" and "To My Nine-Year-Old Self"

Women who look back on their childhood with a mixture of nostalgia and regret is the primary subject of "Material" and "To My Nine-Year-Old Self." In the poems the female speakers experience adulthood in a somewhat negative way and remember their childhood selves with positivity. While Ros Barber views her childhood era as a time when traditions and etiquette facilitated social relations, Helen Dunmore presents her narrator's child self as an unconventional, energetic girl who would "rather leap from a height than anything." Her tomboy days of adventurous activity are remembered with longing and nostalgia.

Ros Barber titles her poem "Material" as she associates her childhood with memories of her mother using the multi-purpose handkerchief which was considered an integral element of a person's life especially if she was female. Her mother used cloth hankies in such profusion that she is wittily nicknamed "the hanky queen" by the speaker. An important figure in the poem, the mother uses the material so often that the speaker-daughter imagines she "had a farm" of handkerchiefs hidden in her dress. An element of humour as well as the use of clever similes and metaphors gives the poem an interesting point of view and imagery. Although Barber uses hyperbole to bring out the virtues of the cloth hankies used in those times, she also projects mixed emotions about this wardrobe essential. While her mother bought her stock of handkerchiefs that she used in such abundance, her daughter, the narrator of the poem, was gifted this item every Christmas whether she liked it or not. Her brothers too received large-sized "male ones ... like they had more snot."

By bringing a commonly used item from her childhood and contrasting it with the "tissue," its modern counterpart, Barber brings in the theme of tradition and modernity, the past versus the present as well as the changed roles of motherhood. The speaker mourns the passing of the hanky, when "those who used to buy them died." With the age of the hanky over, many of the local community events and small friendly businesses that relied on personalized customer relations died as well.

In the modern times the speaker, now a single working mom, lets her children watch TV instead of taking them to participate in talent shows the way her mother did. Comparing herself with her mother, the speaker is conscious of the fact that she has no time to bake biscuits at home. In an unapologetic tone, she admits to having "raised neglected-looking" children, and wonders why she cannot transition to paper tissues when they cost so little?

In contrast to the urban milieu of "Material" consisting of grocery stores and a dancing school, Dunmore's poem is set in a more rural environment, devoid of the city lifestyle, where children have a freer identity, greater access to the outdoors, and lesser gender conditioning. "To My Nine-Year-Old Self" is a dramatic monologue where the middle-aged speaker reflects on her childhood and imagines interacting with her child self, the implied listener. The poem is divided into six irregular stanzas without a rhyme scheme. The tone of the speaker addressing her imaginary child self is conversational and apologetic.

The opening line itself – "You must forgive me" – is a direct address to her younger self who represents a carefree, self-absorbed, and impatient 9-year-old girl. The speaker sees the contrast that age has brought to her – she is more patient, her body has become slower and sedentary. The second stanza continues the note of apology, for having become older, and taking the blame of having "spoiled this body we once shared." The poignancy of trying to make conversation with her young self who is "eager to be gone" makes this poem's speaker appear as if she has lost motivation in her adult life and is perhaps very lonely.

The poem discusses themes of childhood and adulthood and how growing up is not always a pleasant experience. Helen Dunmore uses first and second-person to create the persona of the older woman talking to a young girl and trying to establish a connection where there is none except in the mind of the speaker. The monologue is touching in its speaker's longing for the time gone by, a time of life where every day held promise of an adventure without the responsibilities and the chores that bound adults.

The two poets convey different emotions towards their present, adult lives. While both women personas have problematic lives, Barber's speaker has a distinct preference for her adult self rather than her childhood self when she was smothered by hankies, and by extension, a strong feminine conditioning. She has a nonchalant attitude about the fact that her children lack a constant parental presence in the form of being chaperoned and fed homemade cookies. Barber recognizes that the modern-day single mother is a figure of dissent who does not care to follow prevalent norms of behaviour and etiquette for herself or her children. She, unlike her mother before her, must adjust to the newer realities, and "to do with" the material what she can.

In contrast to Dunmore's narrator who wishes for continued connection with her past but realizes that it is not possible, Barber's narrator rejects nostalgia because it "only makes [her] old." Although she misses the symbols of her childhood and "their soft and hidden mystery," she realizes that she should "let it go." She cannot sacrifice her own ambitions for the sake of being an ideal mother. In the end the speaker comes across as being a self-reliant and empowered woman who is not afraid of passing on these values to her own children.

Barber's title is deliberate and almost synonymous with the word "maternal." The poem, in its initial stanzas, extolls the virtues of traditional mothers who stayed home and made children their priority. In that sense handkerchiefs were symbols of maternal care, and well-raised children. The fact that the older narrator cannot adopt the paper napkins or allow herself to use the cloth versions of her childhood again reinforces her independent spirit and the ability to survive according to her unique circumstances. The poem looks at different forms of motherhood but refrains from privileging one over the other.

In the case of Dunmore's poem, her speaker evinces a protective stance towards the young girl child as if trying to undo their past of adventure when they would impulsively "jump … into the summer morning." Her adult, cautious attitude is the result of the physical damage her body has sustained perhaps due to her youthful mistakes. The narrator also realizes that her younger self does not care about what the future will bring. The lines – "I shan't cloud your morning … I have fears enough for us both" – reveals how different children are from adults. The same person was a completely different person as a child.

As the narrator is a woman, she has fears for her younger self becoming a target of male predators who are "after girl-children." Perhaps Dunmore's poem is a tale of caution told by a woman of experience. The poet's tone is matter-of-fact and resigned, with a minimal use of metaphors to describe the self-absorbed world of the child in contrast to the adult who worries about the future and looks at the past with a mix of longing and regret.

# CHAPTER 7

# Use of Experimental Form and Language in "Look We Have Coming to Dover!" and "Please Hold"

Poetry is a unique literary genre where form, structure, and language come together to create meaning. Poets may choose to use conventional methods to present their themes but if the theme is new, or challenging, then traditional language and poetic modes may not be suitable. Two poems where the poets adopt unusual presentation techniques are "Look We Have Coming to Dover!" and "Please Hold." The poems are, however, dissimilar in their thematic and narrative content.

Daljit Nagra's "Coming to Dover!" portrays the difficult circumstances of illegal Asian immigrants in Britain whose cultural difference and lack of fluency in English pushes them to the margins. O'Driscoll's "Please Hold," highlights how modern technology has altered communication to automated and impersonal modes thus causing users to become frustrated. However, both poems use language in a cacophonic way that effectively conveys the problematic issues.

Nagra's poem is styled in five, five-line stanzas. This apparent regularity is offset by the poet's deliberate mingling of standard and non-standard English, lack of rhyme, dissonance, and an inconsistent point of view. The narrative voice speaks in third-person in the first stanza but from the second stanza onwards the voice shifts to first-person plural. The opening lines suggest the viewpoint of the host country that sees immigrants without means as invaders but welcomes tourists who with their expensive tickets on "cruisers," [lord] "the ministered waves." The difference in language used to describe the stowaways arriving at Dover port versus the tourists arriving at the same destination is deliberate. Standard English is used for the latter while Nagra shows how the non-touristic immigrants are regarded as unwelcome using non-standard, harsh phrases such as "alfresco lash," "brunt," "gobfuls of surf," "phlegmed."

The stowaways are lower down in the hierarchy of Britain's economy in contrast to the tourists who bring in the much-needed revenue. The illegal entrants, in the next stanza, feel rejected even by the country's "seagull and shoal life." The first-person voice is presumably that of the new immigrants exposed to the host country's seagulls that sound angry, and the "yobbish rain" that "unbladders" itself while they make their way inland in a camouflaged manner. Nagra again makes use of non-standard English consisting of misplaced British slang to describe rain and a noun in verb form. Nagra does this to indicate perhaps how Britain perceives these people, or how the immigrants pick up slang to counter their own lack of linguistic fluency that could make their life in Britain easier.

The realism in Nagra's poem exists in tandem with the more obscure images in his poem. This mix of realism, obscurity, and jarring lexis conveys both sides and points of view effectively. From the elitist side, the white Britons view the immigrants as parasites, pests, illegal workers, and people who cannot speak their language properly. From the point of view of the so-called Third World immigrant, England appears inhospitable in its damp and cold climate, but also attracts them as the land of wealth and opportunities – seen in its shiny cars, high rates of employment and a wealthier lifestyle than in their own homeland. The ungrammatical title of the poem conveys this enthusiasm. But the poem describes how this dream of becoming a British citizen remains far-fetched for most immigrants as they remain invisible to the "national eye" or the government for several years.

The middle stanzas in "Coming to Dover!" present the multiple problems faced by immigrants. Their hopes of getting a British passport, suitable housing etc., are belied by the real situation. Illegal immigrants or poor immigrants in general are forced to lead a nomadic existence because jobs are not steady or permanent for them and housing options scarce, thus forcing many to sleep in parks and other unsuitable places. They refer to themselves as "swarms," accepting the sub-human status that has been accorded to them by the dominant culture.

Two images of Britain are presented by Nagra – a Britain that is elite, out of reach, and a Britain that is running on the unseen labour of its immigrant workers. The opening image of the poem with the motorboat arriving in Dover port with tourists on board as well as the stowaways who are later transported under cover of darkness in a van all convey the paradoxical entry points into Britain of migrant citizens hoping for a better life.

In the final stanza, the speaker's voice belongs perhaps to an immigrant who has beaten the odds and gained some visibility and success within the social fabric. Interestingly there is now an element of language fluency and well-being – "Imagine my love and I" – of the narrator drinking at an outdoor cafe and seemingly baptized by the "chalk of Britannia." Whether the final image is a reality or still a dream that every immigrant hopes for is left ambiguous.

Nagra's uses the phrase – "flecked by the chalk of Britannia" – aptly to symbolize the white culture that must be embraced by non-white immigrants in order to become true Britons, whether in the form of the accepted dress code, or drinking wine or speaking the "lingoe" in a grammatically correct form.

The poet's unconventional language use in the poem does include the poetic device of alliteration, especially the repetition of the syllable "s" in the first two stanzas. The poem is also notable for using nouns in verb form – "unbladders", "Blair'd", "passport us to life," "phlegmed" – being a few interesting examples that show how the Nagra's craft in this poem is as important as his content.

Ciaran O'Driscoll's "Please Hold" is a polyphonic text where several voices intersect each other to create a mixed narrative of robotic and human responses. Despite the initial difficulty of identifying who is saying what, the poem is easy to understand in comparison to Nagra's poem with its neologisms, dialect, and non-standard English. "Please Hold" is a common phrase used in telephone etiquette. In the modern world, however, it signifies a long and frustrating wait to get through to a human representative who can answer or solve the customer's problems. With the proliferation of automated communication modes that modern companies adopt for dealing with customer queries, O'Driscoll uses this form of impersonal communication as the title and subject of his poem.

The main speaker in the poem is a man in conversation with a robot, perhaps to solve some problem with his telephone bill. Sensing her husband's impatience at the outset, the wife in the background says that this mode of communication "is the future … and it's the same as the present." The wife's words act as a refrain which is repeated four times in the space of the poem, sometimes in the form of an interruption while the man is getting increasingly angry in his telephone exchange with the robot who is unable to understand his point of view or process his complaint. Despite the robot giving the man "countless options," none of them are suitable.

The form of "Please Hold" is unconventional. It is unstructured in a long dense passage separated by three lines at the end. The poem runs on like a non-stop argument among two or three speakers. O'Driscoll uses repetition, long and short sentences, a refrain, a mix of first-person voices, very simple lexis except when using the title of Mozart's jingle – Aine Kleine Nachtmusik which literally means A Little Night Music when the man is put on hold by the robot. The poem could be seen as mimicking a stand-up comedian's chaotic monologue while the last three lines serve as a more serious epilogue or postscript. By way of context, Mozart composed the jubilant piece of music when he himself was going through a difficult time of his life financially and emotionally, perhaps to lessen his depression.

O'Driscoll's use of Mozart's lightly entertaining piece of music is calculated to provide irony in the poem. The man's frustration at not being heard or being heard wrongly by the robot finally culminates when he is literally put on hold thus increasing his exasperation. The piece of music does not entertain him, in fact it has the opposite effect of making him use taboo language – "Eine fucking Kleine Nachmusic … the robot transfers me to himself."

The use of farce adds to the overall effect of the poem. O'Driscoll differentiates the human and robot voices, but sometimes the human voice sounds robotic. The wife's utterances consist of the same words – "This is the future. We are already there …" giving the quality of emotionless resignation. The robot comes across as a cheerful voice but it can speak and understand only a limited range of vocabulary. One needs to answer in either a "Yes, No, Repeat or Menu." The last option is "Agent" if you want to speak to "someone real, who is just as robotic." The man "scream[s] Agent!" and is "cut off."

The poet's attempt to convey in the form of a poem the helplessness and frustration of the person who must spend hours trying to reach a human representative through automated electronic communication and listen to endless "Please Hold" messages and jingles, is praiseworthy. This is a situation that many can identify with. It is an irony that instead of facilitating customer care, the corporate call system network leads to the public's voice going unheard.

There is a fourth voice in the poem that the man refers to as his translator. This voice translates the robot's messages into what they really mean. O'Driscoll leaves it ambiguous whether the translator is the man's inner voice or if there is indeed a third person in the room. When the robot responds with a mechanical message saying "Your call is important to us," the translator says it means the opposite – "Your call is not important to them."

The fear of being replaced by machines or becoming a clone comes across in the latter half of the poem although it can also be felt through the wife's emotionless monologue. Humans do not count for much anymore. This dark message is put forth more forcefully in the concluding lines that the poet structures in a separate three-line stanza:

> Please hold … Please grow cold … do what you're told … Grow old.
>
> This is the future. Please hold.

The use of two- or three-word sentence fragments gives this stanza a broken and depressing character. By using the word "Please," as an anaphora, the author is pointing out how the word does not necessarily denote politeness if overused. Instead, there is the feeling that electronic communication is cold, calculated and authoritative giving no chance to the user to put in a word. The final lines paint a bleak conformist picture of the modern world with its faceless communication, and overdependence on artificial intelligence thus causing the death and decay of the more human aspects of our civilization.

# CHAPTER 8

# Chaos and the Futility of War in "The War Correspondent"

Ciaran Carson's poems, "Gallipoli" and "Balaclava," included in the longer poem, "The War Correspondent," debunk the idea of war as being necessary or glorious. The first poem details the havoc caused by military operations that turn civilian towns into chaotic, improvised barracks where normal life is turned upside down. In the second poem he brings out the futility of war that jeopardizes lives of young men and that denies them a respectful burial when they die. From a historical perspective, both the Gallipoli campaign in 1915, and the Battle of Balaklava in 1854 were miscalculated military missions that resulted in an unnecessary loss of life.

The poems are filtered through the lens of the war correspondent, a presumably neutral writer or radio commentator who has the task of describing frontline scenes of action. However, Carson gives his speaker/correspondent a greater role than that – the role to shape the listener's/reader's opinion on the two military events that took place.

Although one does not need to know the historical context, Gallipoli, a strategic coastal town in modern Turkey, was used as an encampment by the British and French armies during the Crimean War in 1854 and again during World War I in 1915. The Allied Forces which included also the armies of the Commonwealth nations such as Australia, New Zealand, and India were badly routed in the campaign against the Ottoman Turks. More than 130,000 soldiers died from the Allied side. The Battle of Balaklava on the Crimean Peninsula was a war between the British and the Russian forces that was fought around 1854. Britain's Light Brigade was disseminated as the mission was ill-equipped to face the heavy firing by the vast numbers of Russian infantry on three sides of the valley.

Carson, being of northern Irish descent, perhaps chose these two wars to glorify Britain's war efforts during the colonial era. From the historical perspective, Northern Ireland became a willing part of the United Kingdom while Southern Ireland did not accept British supremacy. The negative reference to the "mewsy lanes of Dublin" in stanza one reveals shades of Carson's subjective approach but beyond this, the poem remains anti-war in general.

The speaker of the first poem, "Gallipoli," tries to describe the town using samples of multiple places. For the sake of his audience who may have never visited Turkey, he asks them to mentally put together a collage of unappealing places familiar to them – Billingsgate fish market in London, the "dirty gutter" of Boulogne, a former British colony, the industrial town of Sheffield, the armoury of Springfield, British warships, etc. – and then asks them to imagine that this "slum" is populated by the Greeks, the Turks, Armenians, and Jews as well as the Arabs, the British and the French. He further requests his audience to imagine dressing this motley group of people – "camel drivers, officers, sailors ... miners, Nubian slaves" – in local outfits such as turbans, shawls, and knickerbockers. To complete the picture, he adds "slaughter houses" for the troops, a hospital as well as a jail. The description conveys improvised and haphazard makeshift structures usually found during wartime, but the visual details carry negative images of the smelly harbour, and the possibility of "cholera" and other diseases induced by the "open sewers," and "flies."

The ten-stanza poem is a mammoth single sentence that uses punctuation and enjambment to create continuity amidst jarring effects. The speaker uses the imperative opening, "Take sheds and stalls," and continues in the same vein, with multiple clauses beginning with "take" until he shifts to another imperative, "then populate this slum," until he shifts to more mellow, invocative openings in the subsequent stanzas. Carson's poem is an example where the form matches the content. The syntactical structure of "Gallipoli" with its numerous semi-colons and commas that cause breaks and pauses reflects the nature of wartime which disrupts the flow of normalcy. Dissonance in the poem not only comes from the war imagery created by the poet but also from the fragmented nature of the narration itself.

Carson also brings in the multi-cultural milieu as a way of intensifying the depiction of the forced Allied occupation of Turkey. The poem represents Gallipoli as a mix of the East and West with the first four stanzas presenting the European aspects and the last six conveying the more eastern flavours as in the references to the "green cantaloupe" and the noise of "multi-lingual squawks of parakeets" that symbolize the unfamiliar tastes and sounds of the place. The adjective "jangly" used by the speaker to describe the local Byzantine music again reflects the biased nature of the reporter.

From a historical perspective the Gallipoli campaign has been described as one of history's worst wartime encampments. To be able to capture these conditions accurately would be an achievement for any war correspondent. The last two stanzas indicate a shift in the voice of the speaker. From the jarring language of the preceding stanzas, the poetic voice emerges in the final two stanzas where the poet uses hyperbole and invocation to convey the terrible effects of war on soldiers of the Allied Powers who lose their strength smoking opium and lie "dead or drunk." The speaker brings in several repelling and graphic images such as dogs searching for dead meat and the "stench of pulped plums." In the end the poet acknowledges that it is extremely difficult to try to "describe Gallipoli." The last line is ironical because the poet has succeeded in the task.

The title Carson chose for his seven-part series, "The War Correspondent," raises some important questions regarding the role of the poet and poetry in war-time conditions. Should the poet be the creator of artistic verse that ignores social and historical events? Or is the poet writer an important commentator on society? Should poetry be escapist or can it provoke political debate? Is the poet merely a recorder of truth or can the poet shape the audience's response to reality? Is war poetry poetic? Is it even possible to poetically render the chaos and futility of war?

The second war poem, "Balaklava," in contrast to the first, is set on the front, in the valley where the British Light Brigade consisting of unarmoured light fast horses, was fired upon on three sides by a Russian regiment of 25,000 soldiers.[1] The poem opens on an ambiguous note with a display of uniformed Turks marching over the same grass where the British

---

1    The suicidal charge, based on miscalculation and misunderstanding, happened during the Crimean War, and is remembered even today thanks to Lord Tennyson's famous poem "Charge of the Light Brigade."

cavalry had been defeated in October 1854. Is the poem about a different event set in a different era? This question is answered in the third stanza. The poem is notable for its semantic field of war with almost every stanza containing references to the military – "firelocks," "bayonets," "infantry," "phalanx," "fifes and drums" are a few examples.

The poet contrasts the colours of the two armies – dark blue against the "light powder blue jackets" of the French regiment mounted on "white Arabs" whose formation is open unlike the rigid lines and columns of the Turks.

The second stanza details the wild flowers growing in abundance in the rich soil of the valley. It is April, the season of spring time, symbolizing youth, and the renewal of life. The war correspondent describes the variety of flowers – red poppies, whitethorn, hollyhocks, and dahlias that have come to life without human intervention. Some soldiers wear the flowers, others "crush" the delicate blooms under their boots, a reminder of how war impacts the psychology of those who partake in it. In contrast to "Gallipoli," this poem privileges the natural world over the human. The soldiers must follow orders of the unseen superior men in control. They have no say in the decision to fight. But whether battles are won or lost, the cycle of life and death goes on.

The poem, made up of four irregular stanzas without a rhyme scheme, has a rich visual spectrum ranging from the dark blue and light blue colours of the uniforms of the French and Turkish armies to the "white Arab" horses, the red colour of the poppies and the green of the meadow. We may wonder whether the war correspondent is hoping to bring the scene to life for his audience, or whether the flowers symbolize the youthful soldiers and the short-lived nature of life itself.

From the third stanza onwards, the commentary shifts to the "phalanxes of rank grass" that are growing on the site of the dead soldiers who fell on 25 October 1854, a direct reference to the British light brigade that was defeated due to heavy firing by the Russian infantry. As the men move through the valley, the horses sense the death that lies on the ground and refuse to "eat those deadly shoots." The last ten lines detail graphic images of the dead – the skeleton of an English soldier, the scarlet tatters of his uniform still "hanging to the bones of his arms."

The regiments of the Turks and French "moved on," over these graves where unbooted "tenants with uncovered bones" lay exposed. The last line is ironical when the war correspondent speaks of the armies sweeping, in rhythm to the military music, over "our fellow men-at-arms" and "half-decayed horses," indifferent to the fate that awaits them.

Carson's two poems are very different in style. While "Gallipoli" conveys the randomness of war-time conditions through its prosaic, fragmented images and clauses, "Balaklava" represents the orderly movement of troops through the beautiful valley in spring season, using poetic imagery. In the second half of the poem, the style changes to a more jarring tone while the speaker describes a landscape that has already seen a battle and left its dead exposed to nature. The reference to the boots and buttons being cut off from the dead soldiers shows how survival in war forces desperate measures and the general lack of compassion or fellow feeling. The images are disturbing and this is reflected in the flow of the words as well.

The war correspondent in both poems goes beyond his role of objective commentator – the poems show the correspondent's negative attitude towards war, the chaos and destruction it causes, and its ultimate futility.

# CHAPTER 9

# A Sense of Place in "The Deliverers" and "You, Shiva, and My Mum"[1]

"The Deliverers" by Tishani Doshi and "You, Shiva, and My Mum" by Ruth Padel invoke a strong sense of place that helps to anchor their poems in terms of physical landscape and cultural rootedness. In both texts the focus is on a woman's journey and India is the main setting in terms of its unique cultural and geographical difference from the world. India in the western imagination is often perceived as a paradoxical space. On the one hand it is seen as an exotic destination for the spiritual traveller; on the other, it is perceived as a backward country ridden with inequalities and poverty. These contradictory perspectives with their correspondent imagery are present in the two poems under discussion.

"The Deliverers," a difficult poem to understand contextually, presents a tough look at India's existing gender bias and the problem of abandoned babies. This problem is not unique to India but abandoning of female babies especially by poor families is specific to the country. Even in modern times gender prejudice in various forms continues to exist across class lines. Doshi creates a three-part poem set in different locales, using graphic imagery with a non-poetic style that is hard-hitting for the reader. In the first stanza the reader is shocked by the disturbing image of a baby girl, buried alive with its head poking out and dug up by a stray dog who thinks the head "was bone or wood, something to chew."

Doshi details the horrific malpractice of female infanticide in her opening lines. A Christian charity mission in Kerala gives shelter to

---

1   Interestingly, Padel's poem was removed from the syllabus for students in Britain as it was deemed too difficult for them to comprehend. It was retained for international students but again removed during the pandemic exam series.

unwanted babies who are left to die, and arranges for their adoption abroad. The narrator's mother is a "deliverer" who transports these babies to their adoptive parents. In this case she takes the girl child to Milwaukee in the United States.

On one level, the poet also questions whether adoption is the answer because the girl grows up at odds from her native culture in a foreign land. The reader wonders whether she is happy. Does she become a whole person or does she feel alienated due to her difference? The poet, in the last section, hints at the girl's search for her origins, perhaps wanting to return to her land of birth. This aspect is left unexplored and ambivalent by Doshi. What is evident is that this young American girl grows up on video tapes, perhaps unable to fit in with her non-biological parental family and extended culture. She searches for her own adoption story, which leads her to watch documentaries about village women and understand patriarchal prejudices against the female infant.

Privileging the male sex in Indian culture is not limited only to Hindu religion although it is more ingrained in its belief systems. The reference to checking the infant for its penis and the absence thereof, decides the fate of the baby. Doshi is perhaps hinting at the extraordinary prominence given to the phallus in Indian culture.

The poem's narration begins in first-person, and shifts to third-person in the last section. The first part of the poem is narrated by the daughter of the woman who transports the baby girl for adoption by an American couple. The child has been traumatized, almost buried alive by her biological mother, this is something her body will always remember on an unconscious level as she will express strange habits at a later stage of her life.

"The Deliverers" presents shifts in both space and time – it opens in the present in India, and moves to the future of the girl child who grows up in America. She, in her turn, metaphorically travels back in time to view cases of female infanticide, a practice which still happens in some parts of India, due to poverty and neglect of the female child.

In this overtly female-centred poem, Doshi shows women as potential murderers and rescuers; as victims, as well as agents of patriarchy and of social change. The title is multivalent – the deliverer can be perceived as the biological mother or the Christian sister who offers shelter to abandoned babies, or the woman who transports them across borders for a better life.

In contrast men are shown in a negative light although no male is present in the poem beyond the faceless "husbands" who inseminate the women with a male or female child.

The poet also categorically privileges American culture in the section where the couple wait at the designated point for the little baby girl to arrive at the airport, unaware that her biological mother almost buried her alive. The poet refers to them positively using words like "ceremony," and "tradition." Waiting is seen as a gesture of respect, order, and restraint, the opposite of impulsive, chaotic behaviour and inhumane acts by the village women in India.

Doshi condemns Indian culture that gives undue prominence to the birth of a male child. It is true that traditional homes celebrate the arrival of a boy baby, but if a family has only female offspring there is usually no cause for celebration as females are perceived as *"paraya dhan"* – wealth that must part from the family in the form of dowries at the time of marriage. This attitude does not exist across the board. Factors such as class, caste, level of income, literacy, rural or urban background, arranged versus love marriage – several factors must be kept in mind before judging this practice or seeing it in generalized terms. Doshi avoids explaining this important information. In consequence the readers form a generalized negative image of India in their minds.

In contrast, Ruth Padel's semi-autobiographical poem[2] avoids highlighting cultural malpractices or social issues and focuses on the personal, celebratory journey of a western woman who spends "a week in the monsoon" season in India. She talks about her elderly mother's experience of attending the marriage of her son to an Indian girl. Reference to Hindu marriage rituals such as Haldi ceremony where the bride is painted with turmeric paste by relatives gives the poem a strong sense of place. Turmeric is used ubiquitously in Indian cuisine and is an important ingredient

---

2    Several online forums support the autobiographical context of the poem. <https://interpreture.com/you-shiva-and-my-mum-poem-analysis/>

according to Ayurveda as it has several medicinal and sacred properties. It is also used for cosmetic purposes in beauty products.

Padel's poem is an ode to Shiva, the Hindu god of destruction of evil and the ego. It is also an ode to her mother who at the age of 80 undertakes a journey through India. The poet delights in her mother's new role of an explorer despite India's rough terrains. The older woman's riding on the motorbike, going through the jungle, experiencing India's remarkable temples and cultural practices is shown in a positive light. Despite her western roots, the mother's embracing of another culture so different from her own is another positive element. The older woman climbing the mountain to the Shiva temple at the end of the poem is an example of western fascination with Indian spirituality. Padel also invokes a third presence – her lover perhaps, or her poetic muse – through whose power she can bring this poem to life.

Like Doshi's poem, Padel's "You, Shiva, and my Mum" contains movement in space and time, although in a more linear fashion. The poem includes references to place names, local flora and fauna, as well as specific cultural practices. The richness of these details – "a leopard-and-leeches path," "full-moon," "a pinky blaze of ribbons, bells, hibiscus," "scarlet henna," "shrine" – add vibrant images to the reader's visual assimilation of India.

The style the poet has chosen in "You, Shiva, and My Mum" is noteworthy. Padel structures the content in the form of four long questions – the poet is asking an unnamed listener if she should share the story of her octogenarian mother's adventures in India. The last line confirms the unknown listener's affirmative response. We can categorize the poem as a dramatic monologue given the presence of an implied listener.

To what extent can the two poems be considered dissenting? Tishani Doshi's strong tone of disapproval permeates the poem, colours her imagery and shapes the readers' response towards India. Her language use does not conform to the traditional poetic expression and instead verges on the graphic and the prosaic. Through her poem she demands reaction from the readers to condemn gender inequality and violence against the female sex in the country.

Padel's "You, Shiva, and my Mum" portrays India as exotic – a land of "the sleeping buffalo," snakes and rock temples – where inner discovery awaits. Overall, the atmosphere of the poem is one of celebration, living with respect for nature, and bonding with one's inner explorative spirit that transcends barriers of nationality and culture.

# CHAPTER 10

# "Out of the Bag" as a Bildungsroman

In Samuel Heaney's poem, "Out of the Bag," the narrator presents a chronological sequence of his personal growth and significant life experiences. The poem begins with the childhood of the young boy narrator and his memories of Doctor Kerlin, the mysterious and intimidating family physician of his childhood who carried out deliveries of babies born at home. This figure continues to influence him into his adulthood. And it is perhaps due to his fascination with Kerlin that the narrator appears to choose the medical profession and assist his own wife's delivery process at the end of the poem.

If we view the poem as a bildungsroman, a story of growth, then it has all the elements of the different stages of life – the visits of the cold and silent doctor, the secretive nature of childbirth, the child's memories of the locked, inaccessible room associated with this important event, the narrator's visit to Greece as a student of medicine, the influence of Greek culture on his psyche, the continued remembrance of Kerlin, the hallucinations, his falling in love, and the last section where his wife becomes a new mother and uses the same euphemistic language as his own mother did when he was a child – "Look what the doctor brought for us all?"

"Out of the Bag," a title that could be taken to mean "a secret that is finally out," brings attention to the many euphemisms that people use in place of direct language. Childbirth is one such event which, until recent times, remained shrouded in mystery, especially for children. Adults commonly used phrases such as the "stork is visiting" or "the stork delivered a baby" or "God has given us a baby" to explain the arrival of a baby. No mention could be made about the actual processes of childbirth or death, for instance.

Heaney's poem begins with the statement – "All of us came in Doctor Kerlin's bag." Presumably this is a child's perspective (conditioned by adults), given in language that seems child-like, with imagery that is drawn from within the house such as "the apron," "the scullery basin," "disinfectant," "spaniel-coloured," etc. This phraseology, however, is intermixed with the more adult memory of how the doctor appeared "like a hypnotist" to the little boy while putting his instruments back into the bag. The boy narrator is curious about childbirth and, simultaneously, intimidated by the doctor, especially by his cold, "Hyperborean," blue eyes.

The poem projects the bag as a symbol for the womb, and by extension, a space of knowledge, life, and birth itself. The narrator views the bag as a curiosity, "a plump ark" that contains all the secrets that he needs to know. The bag, however, is also forbidden territory, a magical space, with its "trap-sprung mouth," signifying ambivalent properties. Another symbol that occurs in the first and last section of the poem is the room where the birthing takes place. The room to the young boy represents a closed space despite his eagerness to know the truth behind childbirth. His young mind obviously disbelieves that babies come in the doctor's bag as he takes careful note of the preparation of hot water, the use of disinfectant, the forceps, and "the chrome surgery tools and blood dreeps in the saw dust." Through the peep holes he can see "infant parts," although not the whole body – "a toe, a foot … an arm, a cock." By comparing the little penis of a newborn to "the rosebud" in the doctor's "buttonhole," Heaney allows the boy narrator to humanize the process of assisted birthing although the use of the "forceps" also suggest the invasive nature of medical practice in traditional birth where the woman was forced to be passive during the process. The "rosebud" also becomes a symbol of life and vitality, a reference to the cycle of life itself as well as a reminder of the boy narrator's fascination with Doctor Kerlin and medicine in general.

The second section of the poem is set away from home, in the world outside, specifically Greece and France, and Heaney includes concrete references to time and location, as well as names of people and buildings to give authenticity to his narrator's personal experiences. The speaker, now a student of both medicine and poetry, finds philosophical knowledge in visiting the healing baths of Epidaurus, a city dedicated to the sanctuaries of the ancient god of medicine, Asclepius. It is interesting that the narrator refers to the influence of Peter Levi, a catholic priest turned poet, and a professor of poetry at Oxford University who also vacationed in Greece several times for health reasons. Heaney brings in alternative paths of healing, including the "cure by poetry," the healing baths, as well as the process of "incubation" where through the ritual of sleep one could meet "the god" of healing. The sanctuaries of Asclepius were the same as modern hospitals in ancient Greece. People of ill-health, including the poet Levi, came from northern Europe to recuperate in the warm Greek sanctuaries and baths.

Heaney makes the transition from childhood to youth a bit abrupt with the change of setting from section one to section two of the poem. The philosophical mood of the narrator in section two nonetheless continues to include the first-person speaker's remembrance of Doctor Kerlin although in a less straightforward way. We are told how the narrator, during a procession in Lourdes, "fainted from the heat and fumes" of incense around him and how this led to him hallucinating about the doctor. The description of the doctor soaping his hands in the scullery basin and drawing cartoon figures with his soapy finger on the steamed-up glass does not appear to have any deep significance until we realize that the narrator is imagining his own birth, his "baby bits" coming together into the doctor's "soapy big hygienic hands." This epiphany marks his strongest connection with Kerlin and his resolve to become a medical practitioner. However, Heaney leaves this for the reader to surmise.

In the third section the narrator sends the sacred grass of the temple to his friends suffering from cancer. We also come to know that he prefers solitude rather than the company of others at the temple in the "midday, mid-May, pre-tourist sunlight." In this section Heaney's use of alliteration and metaphors is notable. In fact, the reader wonders whether the narrator is a poet healer rather than a professional medical student. His attraction towards the Greek temple, and the desire to be visited by Hygeia, the daughter of Asclepius, again brings in the connection to Doctor Kerlin. The reference to Hygeia, the goddess of cleanliness and good health, can be understood as the entry into the next stage of life – marriage and family. This knowledge of wanting union acts as a door opening to the light. In contrast to Kerlin who, in the memory of the child, would darken the door, marriage in metaphorical terms represents "the undarkening door."

The third section is significant because it marks the admission of a strong feminine presence into the narrator's life.

Heaney's long poem is structured in four sections with varying number of stanzas, all of which are three lined. Although the poet uses language in an unconventional manner and rejects the use of rhyme, it fits the highly imaginative nature of his persona, both as a child and as an adult. We see before us, a rounded character, who grows through his experiences and decides his own life trajectories, despite the strong influence of the doctor.

The opening line of the concluding section – "The room I came from and the rest of all of us came from" is very different from the opening of the poem. Heaney is showing us the progress of his child narrator who is now a mature man of knowledge and experience. His world of fantasy has been replaced by "pure reality," where he is more independent and confident. His wife, however, is still trapped in the procedure of the traditional birthing process, where she is either asleep or under heavy sedation. It is unclear in the five stanzas in this section whether the narrator is the doctor or if he is assisting the doctor who is yet to arrive. The narrator is, however, making use of his Greek healing knowledge and is in a state of "incubation" whereby one can commune with God. Perhaps he is about to have another epiphanic moment. What is clear is that the narrator has come full circle – from a timid little boy he has evolved into a mature individual who can midwife his own offspring while his wife still refuses to use direct language and instead prefers euphemistic statements like "And what do you think of the new wee baby the doctor brought for us all when I was asleep?"

Heaney's "Out of the Bag" can be interpreted as a poem of personal growth but it also raises ideas of how doctors are viewed as God in some cultures since they exercise so much power. Another issue seen in the poem is how women's bodies and minds in patriarchal cultures are suppressed. Even during childbirth, a woman is expected to subject herself to patriarchal control, and is not allowed to express herself or be an active participant in the birth of her child.

Despite the logical sequence of events given in the poem, Heaney's narrator is not exactly a normal young man. The middle sections show us a person who is irrational, and overly imaginative and passionate to be fit for the medical profession. He suffers from hallucinations, loves solitude, and is obsessed with a person from his childhood. He appears to be a high-strung individual. Due to these factors, the poem consists of several levels of ambiguity which makes it difficult to interpret.

# CHAPTER 11

# Female Selfhood and Empowerment in "The Furthest Distances I've Travelled" and "Map Woman"[1]

A search for selfhood lies at the core of "Map Woman" by Carol Ann Duffy and "The Furthest Distances I've Travelled" by Leontia Flynn. Both poems are women-centred and present travel as a mode of gaining self-reliance and independence.

"Map Woman" is about a young woman aspiring for a future that is different and more exciting than her circumscribed childhood and youth in a small town. The poet uses the metaphor of a map to show how her provincial background is ingrained in her and printed on her skin like a tattoo. She cannot escape it; it always seems to define her, and hold her back. The third-person narration, interspersed with second-person observations, details this woman's yearning for selfhood and fulfilment – to travel to distant cities, to get married, and to start her life. Instead, her only escapes are to watch the cinema and wave out at train passengers passing through her small town to faraway exotic places. The poet describes her life as "waiting for time to start … your tiny face trapped in the window's bottle-thick glass like a fly."

In contrast to the confined predicament of the woman in Duffy's poem, the first-person narrator in "The Furthest Distances" is cheerful and free. She details her travelling adventures to remote places like Croatia and Siberia and unlike the inexperienced woman in "Map Woman," this woman has left the stability of her home and is already in control of where she wants to go. Her voice remains personal throughout the monologue by the insistent use of "I"-implying her self-reliant approach to life. She affirms travel – "Yes. This is how to live" – and enjoys her carefree lifestyle.

---

1    The "Map Woman" was removed from the exam series in 2020.

In the third stanza it becomes clear to her that her future lay in "restlessness" and "anonymity." The latter word choice gives the reader the idea that the young woman rejects a structured life, and instead is happy to experience the excitement of a nomadic, rootless existence, where the self is not defined by one's name or a fixed address.

The map woman too craves restlessness. She hopes to escape her small-town roots by travelling to unknown places but is held back by multiple fears – the fear of her body map being visible to others, the fear of taking the "motorway" described by Duffy as the "roaring river of metal." At this point the woman also fears taking a risk as she has heard reports of young female hitchhikers being kidnapped. There is a hint that she has a deep fear of her father who was probably abusive in her childhood. In order to gain some confidence, she first hides her skin under layers of clothing when she is in the public eye. At home she tries to scrub out the "prison and hospital stamped on her back." Nothing helps. The need to rid herself of her past gets stronger until the readers are informed in the seventh stanza that the map woman has finally left her home town – "she lived down south, abroad, en route, up north ... in hotels, in the back of cabs ..." These multiple journeys mark a major shift towards her more independent self.

Flynn's "The Furthest Distances" can be categorized as a travel poem given its obvious title. However, rather than only focusing on the physical aspects of travelling, Flynn explores travel in metaphorical terms as well. With poetic techniques, imagery and lexical choices, the poet reveals the narrator's emotional and personal growth thus far in her journey of life and the philosophical realizations she has reached.

In the initial lines, the narrator begins by describing the early days when she started travelling and adventuring. "Like many folk, when first I saddled a rucksack" indicates that travelling is an act of both exhilaration as well as responsibility. The metaphor highlights the unusual yoking of the body to the baggage which is typical of solo travellers. The phrase also draws our attention to budget travelling where the big, heavy rucksack with its multiple pockets and strappings contains all the essentials one could need for camping.

Flynn's narrator enjoys travel, and believes life can be lived to the fullest "on the beaten track, the sherpa pass, between/Krakow/and Zagreb, or the Siberian white/cells of scattered airports." There is a certain ambiguity regarding the colour choice given to airports – it is unclear whether airports are being compared to prison cells due to their seclusion from the outside world. The whiteness implies an absence of colour and by extension, the absence of the real world of travel that can be experienced on simpler modes of transport such as the Greyhound or backpacking rather than on the cold, sanitized airplanes.

Duffy's heroine in "Map Woman" is an emotionally different character from the narrator in "The Furthest Distances." The first woman is trying to escape "the one-way street of her past" through whatever means possible, while the second has perhaps become directionless in her search for anonymity. Both are, however, seeking self-fulfilment and validation through their travel experiences.

Once the map woman is on the move, she no longer has the stability of her home or the safety of her town. Her new professional identity brings her wealth but it is unclear as to what her job really is. She now sleeps in cabs, motels, or airplanes. She does not share details but it seems she has chosen a profession where she acts as an escort with lovers paying for her travel and living expenses. Duffy's protagonist wears expensive clothes and perfumes, rides in limousines, and makes love in the dark, always conscious of how the lover "caressed the map ... from north to south."

At the end of the poem with nowhere else to travel to, she decides to drive back to her home town. She is now rich enough to get a room "with a view," but she discovers that the town is no longer the same. Streets have new names now and walkways are no longer familiar so much so that she loses her way. Perhaps in consequence to this development, that night her skin map sloughs off like a ghostly dress and in the morning her body has no mark. Swiftly she leaves behind her old, mapped self on the floor of the hotel room, checks out, and gets behind the wheel. However, as she drives away, her skin begins to itch and stretch, the old streets begin tunnelling from beneath as if "hunting for home." Duffy gives sinister significance to the last three words. To hunt is an aggressive act, and in this case the skin of the woman is a living organ with a mind of its own. It is painful to be at odds with oneself, perhaps the map woman has become fragmented and divided because her skin felt as if it "belonged" to another person.

Duffy uses several metaphors and similes in this long poem. The use of enjambment gives the poem an unpredictable flow from one stanza to the next, the reader does not know what is coming. The poem is dramatic and suspenseful; it has all the ingredients of a thriller to keep the reader engaged. In the last stanza she uses a variety of metaphors to describe her old peeled skin. She calls it a "shroud," and a "small ghost." Her attempts to run away from her old self and her origins, however, fail. The map resurfaces on her skin, thus claiming her identity forever.

Flynn's poem also ends in pessimism and a sense of failure. The woman traveller has been on two parallel journeys, one physical and the other metaphorical. Her love relationships, for instance, can be seen as emotional journeys where she has "holidayed briefly" in someone's life. The temporary nature of love is painful due to the "routine evictions" one is subjected to, like checking out of a motel, where one leaves behind souvenirs for others to find. What one carries away as memories gives it a positive power. However, the woman talks about the "crushed valentines" being symbols of lost love and regret.

Both women yearn for relationships but not at the cost of their freedom. This idea is brought out in the early part of "Map Woman" where the woman sits outside the church watching wedded couples exit with rings on their fingers and wishes for her own marriage. However, in her life she has a series of lovers with whom she travels to different places. In the end both women are lonely and have reached a state of self-realization.

Regardless of the failure that each woman experiences in her own way, the poets portray their individualized female personas with courage and strength. They grow through their experiences instead of remaining one-dimensional figures trapped in a static life forever.

# CHAPTER 12

# Murder and Psychosis in "The Lammas Hireling" and "Giuseppe"

A cold-blooded murder of an innocent being is at the heart of "The Lammas Hireling" by Ian Duhig and "Giuseppe" by Roderick Ford. The poems offer portraits of aggressors who have a psychotic mentality and are ruthless as a consequence. While Duhig's poem is in first-person and reconstructs the bizarre monologue of a dairy farmer who confesses to committing multiple murders, Roderick's poem recounts a symbolic killing during wartime so that the starving troops can be fed. Both poems function within a context of morality by bringing in issues of ethics and guilt as well as referring to God or a divine representative at some point in the narrative.

"The Lammas Hireling" opens in an innocuous way although the use of Irish dialect and mythology at times gives rise to problems in interpretations from the beginning. A farmer buys a bull at a Christian Lammas annual fair that is held in August in Ireland and England. At such fairs one could buy traditional foods and livestock among other things.[1] He is happy with his purchase because he was so "cheap." The line "I'd still a light heart and a heavy purse," appears to make no sense unless we understand it as the farmer still having a light heart and a purse full of money despite the cost of the bull. In the six lines of stanza one we are told how the cows loved the bull and that the milk production doubled. While the bull is at the farm, the cows "dropped heifers, fat as cream."

This interpretation is easy but it starts to get problematic in the second stanza when the farmer, having a nightmare one night about his "dear late wife," goes to the barn where the bull is referred to as naked wearing "leather

---

1    &lt;https://en.wikipedia.org/wiki/Ould_Lammas_Fair&gt;

horns." He kills this creature in the third stanza imagining him to be the human lover of his dead wife. While some readers accept the fact that the farmer buys a bull from the fair, others contest this interpretation and say that the farmer actually hires a man to take care of his cattle. The latter theory is supported by the title, "The Lammas Hireling,"[2] but the poem does state explicitly that the farmer "buys" the "he" figure. One cannot purchase a hireling because they would be given weekly wages.

There are several logical problems even if we accept the hireling interpretation. The farmer finds a "pale form" under the dim light of the lantern, probably in the barn. Why would the hireling be standing naked in the middle of the night in the barn where the cattle are kept? And why would a fox-trap be around the man's ankle? It is more feasible for an animal to walk into a fox-trap than a full-grown farm worker. Perhaps the answers to these questions are meant to shake the poem's logical underpinnings.

Instead of trying to pin down the logical facts of what happens in the narrative, it is more significant to understand the mental instability of the persona that Duhig has created. The speaker is not a normal person – he probably also murdered his wife in the recent past. The fact that he is haunted by dreams of his wife could point to his guilt. The "torn" voice of his late wife could be reminding him of her dying moment or it could also refer to the sound she made during the sexual act. The farmer imagines the creature in the barn as a "warlock," a magical being who can change their shape. In the heat of the moment, he forgets wisdom, and shoots the poor animal or man "through the heart."

Following the gun shot, the hireling changes into a hare. This event lessens the farmer's guilt as he rationalizes that he has only killed an animal and not a human. Again, the psychotic imagination of the farmer visualizes the corpse decaying at a rapid rate and imagines him "fur over like a stone mossing." He throws the sack containing the body over the bridge and into the river. The fact that the farmer hears no "splash" again convinces him that he did the right thing by killing a "warlock."

---

2    <https://blogasenglish.wordpress.com/2016/03/03/the-lammas-hireling-revis ion-notes/>

But killing innocent people or taking the law in your own hands has consequences. "Now my herd's elf-shot" – the farmer finds that a curse has fallen on his cattle and that his life is ruined. He shares this information with the priest as a confession – "Bless me Father, I have sinned." The ending comes as a shock to the reader because traditionally a Catholic confession opens with the line – "Forgive me, Father, for I have sinned," but the poet has chosen the American version with "Bless me, Father …." Duhig subverts the traditional structure of a confession by putting the first line last. The presence of a listener is only revealed in the end of the poem, thereby bringing in an element of surprise or shock. The speaker is clearly psychotic as it has only been sixty minutes since his previous confession. Is a guilty consciousness pushing him to repeatedly confess or is he changing his story with every confession?

The ending of the dramatic monologue shows that the farmer can no longer be a productive member of society. He spends his nights "casting balls from half-crowns," or in other words, making bullets for his gun, and his days in the church doing confession. The poem's ambiguity can be traced to the instability of the speaker's utterances and, also to the inclusion of magical folklore that challenge the reader's expectations. On a structural level, Duhig's poem is a short four-stanza poem that makes use of enjambment to create both flow and disruption in the text. The monologue tells us less about the hireling, who has no voice in the poem, and more about the demented man who killed him for no cause.

"Giuseppe" is also a short poem in free verse without rhyme or rhythm that narrates a story of senseless violence and murder of the "only captive mermaid in the world" during World War II. Like "The Lammas Hireling," the poem tests the reader's belief and is also in the form of a confession told by Giuseppe, the aquarium keeper, to his nephew, the first-person narrator. The poem opens in an anecdotal manner describing a time in Sicily during the Second World War and a place "where the bougainvillea grows so well." The reader is unprepared for the next line which relates how an innocent mermaid "was butchered." The irony of the pleasant Mediterranean setting contrasting with the heinous crime is deliberate and meant to shock the reader.

The uncle then goes on to divulge details of who authorized this crime. Using common names of the "doctor, a fishmonger" and a "priest," Ford makes clear the patriarchal nature of society that allowed the murder of a pregnant mermaid who is not a given a voice in the poem perhaps to accentuate her lack of status or identity. The oppressors rationalize her killing. Since she cannot speak the language of humans, she is regarded as "only a fish" and therefore a subhuman.

Like Duhig's "The Lammas Hireling," Ford's poem also encourages more than one interpretation. Are we to see the mermaid's murder as an isolated incident or are we to see it as being symbolic of systemic war crimes against the underprivileged or voiceless sections of civilian society? Is the mermaid real or does she represent the female sex in general? What is the role of Uncle Giuseppe – is he a participant in the crime or an observer?

Although it is unclear whether the aquarium keeper kills the mermaid or whether the killing is carried out by the fishmonger, their complicity in the act can be surmised from the fact that they carry out the orders from their superiors and do not protest. The priest who holds the hands of the mermaid while she is being slaughtered rationalizes that a fish "cannot speak," but in actuality "she screamed like a woman in terrible fear." These words are uttered by Uncle Giuseppe, who was probably a spectator, but who cannot erase this frightful event from his memory and shares it with his nephew.

The major part of the poem is about the mermaid's questionable human status – is she a fish or a woman? The doctor states that she cannot be human because he removes her "ripe, golden roe" and shows it as a "proof" that "she was just a fish." The fact that she is wearing a ring on her hand is not considered. In stanza four, the perpetrators perform a burial where the "head and hands" of the mermaid are put in a box thus signifying that she was partly human.

The illogical rationalizations uttered by the killers match those of the farmer who also kills an innocent being and thinks of it as a fantasy animal that deserved to die in "The Lammas Hireling." However, the context of the killing in "Giuseppe" is wartime when the troops were starving and food had to be arranged. This reason appears like another rationalization behind the senseless murder of the vulnerable creature. The soldiers are fed the cooked meat and told that "a large fish was found on the beach."

Ford explores the effects of the crime on the aggressors' mental peace. The doctor who removed the roe refuses to eat when the egg is "offered to him." The priest tries to show sympathy by holding the hand of the mermaid but is sickened by her screams. The uncle who tells this confessional tale cannot look at his nephew "in the eye," thus showing his feelings of guilt and complicity. The "certain others" who authorized the slaughter are not named by the keeper but they could be the military commanders. There are also those who try to loot the ring from the body before its burial but they are "stopped."

In "Guiseppe," Ford brings in themes of patriarchy as well as war crimes against the weak and the vulnerable. Questions about women's lack of defence or control over their bodies and the rape and looting of innocents allowed during war are also raised in the poem. Ford's inclusion of a fantasy element of a pregnant mermaid is similar to Duhig's portrait of a warlock shape-shifting into a hare. Their main intention, however, appears to be in exposing the psychosis that afflicts men when they are in positions of power and authority.

# CHAPTER 13

# Caregiving in "A Minor Role" and "On Her Blindness"

Coping with one's own life-threatening illness or caring for a family member with a serious disability is the subject of "A Minor Role" by UA Fanthorpe and "On Her Blindness" by Adam Thorpe. Although the two poems differ in the situations they describe, they share a personal glimpse into dealing with health issues that are often kept secret from the outside world. Thorpe's poem is autobiographical and focuses on his relationship with his blind mother during the final years of her life. Fanthorpe's poem is more symbolic and portrays how life is lived on two levels – the public and the private. This gets more problematic when one is suffering from a terminal condition or looking after someone who is, and does not want to share details about it. The poem reveals how playing a role in a social setting is different from being oneself at home where there are fewer expectations. This demarcation between the private and the public self is evident in most people's lives and both poems focus on this aspect in varying degrees.

"On Her Blindness" is straightforward and written in a conversational style using twenty-two non-rhyming couplets and a single-line stanza at the conclusion. The vocabulary is simple and casual for the most part. The poet describes the terrible predicament of his mother who has lost her sight and who calls the experience a "living hell." The use of "speech" within the poem lends it a more personal touch and makes the character of the mother more credible and authentic.[1] However, her self-revelation is only shared with her son and no one else. In public she does not let her disability define her or limit her. Thorpe, himself, shares that his mother could "not

---

[1]  <https://interpreture.com/on-her-blindness-poem-analysis/>

bear being blind" but that usually one does not hear such sentiments as
one is supposed to keep up public appearances and "bear it like a Roman."

The poem portrays the mother as a strong woman with hope and dig-
nity. At home when she bumps into things, her husband jokes that she is
without a "built-in compass." However, she takes it in her stride and con-
tinues to act as if she can see, and even smiles at the drawings made by her
grandchildren. The poet's mother keeps up her social life and continues
to drive her car and visit exhibitions and even watch television "the wrong
way." The fact that she still has hope in a cure for her blindness keeps her
from ending her life. This information shared with her son shows how
close she feels to him. The poet, however, calls himself an "inadequate"
son who is unable to respond in an empathetic manner. In the final week
of her life when she is in hospital, he tells her about the vibrant autumn
colours outside, forgetting that she cannot see but hoping to cheer her up.
She is too frail to move but she acknowledges that "it's lovely out there."

Adam Thorpe's portrait of his mother is understated, yet it is reflective
of a warm and generous woman who wants to experience life in all its col-
ours and textures but who is denied the use of her sight. Instead of making
a fuss or complaining to her immediate family, she "pretended to ignore
the void," and get on with her day-to-day life. This could be her coping
mechanism to be regarded as normal as possible. That her family forgot
at times of her disability proves how much she had adapted to act in a way
that was her usual, pre-blind self.

The ending of the poem is poignant with Thorpe's emotions on the
death and loss of his mother. He hopes that with death, she found her
sight, and that "she was watching, somewhere, in the end." The last line
comes as a surprise because we, as readers, are unprepared for it. A poem
that talks about the ordinary aspects of a person's life and then suddenly
takes it to a symbolic level jolts the expectations of the reader. Perhaps
this is why the last stanza is only composed of a single line so that it makes
a greater impact.

Overall, the poem talks of literal blindness, but in the end, Thorpe gives
it a metaphorical twist – the gaining of inner sight after death would be a
gift that his mother could enjoy. In this way, the poem becomes a narrative
of positivity and hope in keeping with his mother's character.

In contrast to Thorpe's poem, Fanthorpe's "A Minor Role" is less straightforward and more ambivalent. She opens the poem using the metaphor of life being a "stage" where one enacts different roles. This is a common metaphor used by writers. Even the title corroborates the view that life can be seen as a symbolic stage where some people perform central roles while others may play less significant ones. In the poem, however, the poet may be using the stage metaphor to symbolize the public roles that one adopts or the literal minor roles the speaker has been asked to perform – "propping a spear" or acting the "servant" part. These so-called minor roles are, however, quite significant, because if there are even small mistakes, "the monstrous fabric" of the show can draw the audience's "sniggers."

One wonders with the second stanza whether the poet is continuing the life-is-a-stage analogy – the play within the poem – or is she referring to real life situations? The speaker desires public roles where she is "unobtrusive," or not prominent. She likes the "waiting-room roles" where she may be taking a friend to a doctor's office, comforting him or her by "holding hands under veteran magazines," being friendly with the receptionists, and in general, "sustaining the background music of civility." Here we are confronted with the idea of how real life requires us to put on a mask of politeness and civility in order to get things done, especially within the context of doctors and treatments. It also refers to the "background" or behind-the-scene assistance that one can give for the larger show to go on. Fanthorpe uses two semantic fields within the first and second stanzas, that of the theatre where elements of drama are revealed through words such as "entrances and exits," for instance. On another level we are given the hospital lexis through vocabulary choices such as "dosages," "consultants' monologues," etc.

With the third stanza that begins paradoxically with "At home in the street," which can refer to both the private and public spaces, the poet addresses the general reader in the second-person, establishing a personal connection with the phrase "you may see me." The speaker talks of dodging people to whose intrusive health queries she gives concise and polite formulaic answers – "O, getting on, getting better."

The difference between the social, polite public self and the more honest private self comes up in the fourth stanza when the speaker is at home trying to cope with the uncomfortable reality around her. Fanthorpe leaves it ambiguous whether the speaker is talking about her own illness or someone else's. There is no proof in the poem that the speaker is referring specifically to her own illness. To make a meal for a "hunger-striker," could also refer to a sick family member who does not want to eat. The stress on the caregiver is sometimes as great as the struggle to cope with one's own illness.

Some critical material on the poem categorizes it as autobiographical but unlike "On Her Blindness" where the poet's name "Adam" is used in the twelfth line, "A Minor Role" makes no direct reference to UA Fanthorpe's name or life specifically. Yet some commentaries assume this casual connection to the poet's life by bringing in facts about Fanthorpe's career as "a receptionist at a psychiatric hospital".[2] Another point to bear in mind is that the poems are meant to be examined for their internal content and context rather than exclusively within the poet's external biographical context.

Despite the difficulty of interpreting whose illness is being talked about, in stanza five we are told that being sick or looking after someone who is sick is not an easy journey. Sometimes one could wish "for a simpler illness like a broken leg" but in the end a positive attitude will help instead of "tears" or "lassitude."

Whether Fanthorpe wrote this poem inspired by her own work experiences as a hospital receptionist or not, what is more important is how she presents the role of the caregiver as a major, not a minor role. To be behind the scenes, propping up the patient in all respects requires courage and patience. The final line of the last stanza – "I'm here to make you believe in life" – is not a minor role at all. In fact, without it the whole "fabric" of a terminally-ill person's life could collapse.

The title then can be seen as ironic where the poet means the opposite to what is being said. When someone with a serious medical problem must suffer delays and be referred to multiple doctors, the role of the caregiver becomes significant. It is not a "star part" because one does not get rewarded or recognized for it. The narrator, in fact, dissents with "the terrible drone

---

2    <https://blogasenglish.wordpress.com/2016/03/09/a-minor-role-ua-fanthorpe/>

of the Chorus," a reference to the commentator role played by the elders in ancient Greek tragic dramas which usually had sad endings.

Like "On Her Blindness," "A Minor Role" too ends with a one-liner which is as forceful as the previous poem's ending – "I am here to make you believe in life." This philosophy of Fanthorpe's narrator may be pointing to the difference between art and life. One can die a false death on stage but in real life there are no second chances. We have only one life and we must try to hope for a productive future despite the challenges of complex illnesses.

# CHAPTER 14

# Race and Class in "Song" and "Fantasia on a Theme of James Wright"[1]

"Song," by George Szirtes is a poetic portrayal of a revolutionary movement where the power of a leader in catalyzing resistance against racial injustice is the main subject. Using melody and simple rhyme, the poet dedicates this poem to South African anti-apartheid liberal parliamentarian named Helen Suzman who spoke out against white supremacy and sought equal rights for Africans in their own home-land during the 1960s and 1970s. Sean O' Brien in his poem, "Fantasia on a theme of James Wright," highlights the oppression of miners whose work takes them down treacherous underground tunnels, devoid of fresh air and sunshine, for long hours of each day. He describes the plight of these working-class men who die while harvesting coal for factories owned by the rich classes and yet no one gives them recognition for their hard work. Both poems use poetic features such as assonance, rhyme, and melody to draw attention to the violation of basic human rights. While "Song" is a poem of hope, "Fantasia on a Theme" is an elegy for the exploited and forgotten dead miners "singing … inside the earth."

"Song" uses repetition and a deliberately simple lexis to draw the reader into the poem. "Nothing happens until something does" – the opening line which is also the refrain, introduces us to the subject of how the oppressed race continues to bear injustice until someone takes up their cause and fights the dominant system. The power of a single voice of dissent, in

---

1    Both these poems were removed from the syllabus during the pandemic exam series.

this case a woman's, according to Szirtes, is enough to mobilize the masses and make them aware of their ability to change the status quo.

In Sean O'Brien's poem, the injustices suffered by the mining workers and their families are shown through symbolism and dark imagery – the miners, we are told, are "labouring still" in the "black pools" and "underground rivers." Using the techniques of the Deep Image Poetry developed by poets like James Wright, O'Brien creates compelling images that shape the reader's sympathies towards the underprivileged mining community. One such intertextual image reference is to an actual painting created in 1888 by Ralph Hedley titled "Coming Home," showing two miners returning through the village at dusk. O'Brien mentions that the "tiny" walkways in the vast underground "estate" are decorated with the prints of this painting but that the world is not aware of these people. In other words, the miners and their life are invisible to the world.

Both poets strongly identify with the oppressed and their need for their voices to be heard. O'Brien refers to the miners as his "brothers" but his tone remains resigned as history has never recognized the value of the poor; it has only recorded events of earth-shaking importance, and "not the thud of iron doors sealed once for all." He develops the theme of suffering by giving examples of how the miners die due to sudden flooding or due to ingesting great amounts of coal dust. The mix of concrete and abstract nouns gives the poem a realistic as well as a philosophical context.

In both poems the idea of the centre versus the margin is present where the centre represents a position of dominance. The centre in O'Brien's poem is the rich or the upper classes who run their factories with the coal that is painstakingly mined by the workers in damp tunnels and underground shafts. The centre in "Song" is the white, dominant race that makes unequal laws. The people who represent the margin are far from the centre, in fact quite invisible, just like the Africans who were brutalized and shorn of their basic human rights during apartheid or the miners who spent years of their life inside the earth rather than out in the open air, living healthy lives. Szirtes, however, takes the example of South Africa and shows how the margins can be united to overthrow the power of the centre.

The title of O'Brien's poem refers to James Wright, the American poet who propounded the genre of Deep Image Poetry, a form where the poem's images generate the meanings. This kind of poetry was generally "resonant, stylized, heroic."[2] Wright was born in an industrial town of Ohio and was known to experiment with language and style. We can find O'Brien using the techniques of Deep Image Poetry in "Fantasia on a Theme" in terms of a distinct structural pattern of three lines in every stanza. The lexis in the poem is lyrical with a melancholic musical alliterative quality that comes through phrases such as "black-braided banners." The poet presents realistic images of the miners "gargling dust" that seem at the same time deeply symbolic of the hazards that they experience daily. On the abstract level as well, O'Brien impresses the readers with his poignant and ironic portrayal of "a class immortalized by want."

O'Brien's poem, as already mentioned, is a mix of the abstract and the concrete, the latter being more symbolic than real. The language in the poem is passive and reflective but some words do denote the continuing futile endeavours of the miners. The ominous sounds of onomatopoeia ("thud") reinforce the bleakness of the miners' situation in the sixth stanza. Szirtes, in contrast to O'Brien, uses rhyming active verbs to denote the movement of the masses, such as "break," "shake," "shift" and "lift." Just as a machine becomes functional once all the parts work in unison, similarly people can come together as a force to bring about change. The anti-apartheid movement was inspired by Gandhi's non-violent struggle for independence in India. The title of the poem aptly suggests how political fights can be won through a harmless song or "distant buzz" that can galvanize people into solidarity.

The visual qualities of both poems are noteworthy. Szirtes uses the extended metaphor of a machine whose every part, however small, can work in harmony with the pivot, to make things happen – such as a revolution. Using synecdoche – "small hands" and the contrasting adjectives – "small" versus "monstrous," the poet brings in the idea of power and powerlessness. He refers to Suzman's lone voice in the parliamentarian debates when he says "one pale feather tip the balance on a sinking ship." Using alternative rhymes, Szirtes uses melody to create a song of revolution where the oppressed class can "oppose" the weight by which are "crushed the broken voices of the hushed." The silenced voices belonged to the African people

2   <https://en.wikipedia.org/wiki/Deep_image>

who were dominated by the more vocal power of the white minority. The hope that runs through "Song" is drawn from the choice of lexis used by the poet to denote the power that can be wielded by "however small the hand." Once the wheel is set rolling, the poet affirms that the "Earth may be made to move."

In contrast, an atmosphere of pessimism permeates "Fantasia on a Theme" – the oppression, poverty and general neglect of the coal miners will continue while the world moves on. The "singing of the dead" represents the dead voices of the thousands of miners that have sacrificed their lives due to hazardous work conditions and that will go unnoticed by the living. The final line – "matters will never be otherwise" – reveals the degree of the poet's sadness and resignation.

The two poems are similar in that they use song and music to convey their themes. However, the songs sung by the dead miners are perhaps a reminder of the actual songs they sung while at work. The songs brought an element of cheer into their monotonous lives. The title of Szirtes's poem can be taken to mean "harmony" and oneness that is essential to drive a movement to its goal. "Song" could also refer to the songs of resistance created by enslaved peoples all over the world during the imperialist era. Both poems acknowledge the existence of the unsung heroes who sacrifice their individual desires or lives for the sake of the common goal. "Fantasia" is taken to mean a piece of music but it could mean also a dream, a fantasy created by the poet while being inspired by James Wright.

Music carries within it the ability to touch and mobilize people. Both poets use this element not only in their use of lyrical language but also in their political message. Music, whether joyful or melancholic, can create empathy and unity.

# CHAPTER 15

# Synecdoche in "Genetics" and "Effects"

In both "Genetics" and "Effects" the poets use the "hand" to represent the person being referred to. Sinead Morrissey's speaker sees her parents in the shape of her hands, while Alan Jenkins' persona draws a portrait of his mother while holding her "scarred" lifeless, hand. The use of the part to represent the whole is a primary literary device used in both poems and therefore the synecdoche becomes central to understanding both the symbolism and the content of the two poems.[1] While "Genetics" celebrates a life of commitment and companionship, "Effects" focuses on the breaking down of family ties and the loss of a parent. Both poems are first-person narrations although the mood and structure are widely different.

"Genetics" is a short, rhythmic villanelle that delivers a powerful message of love and union between two human beings through the birth of their child. The title itself celebrates the biological connection between parents and their children. Whether the parental marriage lasts or not, in the child, according to the poet, that relationship still lives and perpetuates itself. "Genetics" talks about the physical traits the speaker has inherited from her parents just by looking at her hands and noting that her father is present in the shape of her fingers and her mother "in her palms." The poet shows how one can trace one's connections to one's parents merely by looking at the features of one's own body. In this way, our genetics makes it impossible to break away from or disown our family origins.

In "Effects," however, Jenkins focuses on the son who left his dying, alcoholic mother in a psychiatric hospital despite her need for his presence in her life. In the poem, the son holds the hand of his dead mother

---

1   <https://www.merriam-webster.com/words-at-play/synecdoche-metonymy-usage-differences>

and through it remembers her tough life of being a wife and mother in a working-class family. A poem of guilt and regret, "Effects," reveals the bond between a mother and her son and how children move away from home and are unable to value their parents until it is too late. This realization indirectly comes to the narrator while holding his mother's hand, when she is no more.

Within the context of the modern family where individualism often leads to conflict and divorce, Sinead Morrisey talks about honouring the collective heritage of one's parents even when "nothing is left of their togetherness." Her speaker takes the metaphor of the hands where the fingers resemble her father's and the palm reminds her of her mother. Although the fingers and the palms are separate elements, together they form the hands that symbolize the identity of the child. When the palms are brought together to make a "steeple," the narrator uses the hands to represent the "marriage register" of the parents. To create a child is a sacred act, according to Morrissey. The narrator's semi-religious ideas are conveyed through the distinct word choices. The narrator can be presumed to be female although there is nothing in the poem that can prove that the speaker is a woman and not a man.

Celebrating the cycle of life is another idea that is present in the poem. Marriage, love, commitment, and procreation is the subject of "Genetics." The narrator identifies with her parents and wants to experience togetherness in her own life. In the end she asks her lover to take her with him, and "take up the skin's demands for mirroring in bodies of the future." She wishes for them to come together and create their child in whose body they will "mirror" their own union and live on.

Despite her parents' separation, their "other lovers," the narrator cannot cut her ties from them as they continue to "touch [her] where fingers link to palms." In her hands, their marriage or union is still intact. The poem is a dramatic monologue by virtue of there being a listener, the man the narrator addresses as her lover in the last stanza. The vocabulary range is simple and yet conveys lexis from different semantic fields such as the human anatomy, the church, and marriage. Morrissey's rhyme scheme of aba cdc is also musical, lending the poem a mood of optimism and joy.

In contrast, Jenkins' "Effects" is a dark poem in free verse, lacking stanza breaks. The continuous thought process arising from the memories of his dead mother as the speaker holds her hand does not allow for separate stanzas. The fifty-line poem could have been evenly divided into five ten-line stanzas but Jenkins' use of run-on sentences, and the inclusion of multiple clauses would have made this impossible as there are only two complete sentences in the whole poem.

The central image of the hand acts as its cohesive factor – the son holding the hand of the mother he abandoned. The poet describes her hands in the context of her life, a life that was made up of difficult kitchen chores – "chopping, slicing, … scrubbing." The mother's portrait through the synecdoche of her hands paints the character of a woman who had to keep the home clean and create meals for her family within a limited budget. The rings his mother wore, and her "Classic ladies" watch are also examples of metonymy because they can be associated with her traditional life and marriage.

"Genetics" and "Effects" offer somewhat similar portraits of parental relationships. In the former poem, the marriage is based on love although it ends in separation, later. The marriage described in "Effects" is not that strong as the mother stops wearing her wedding rings while her husband was alive indicating that she may not have been on good terms with him anymore. Ironically, she misses him after his death, and puts the rings back on to let "everyone know that she was his wife." The mother also develops an alcohol addiction – it becomes "her way to be with [her husband] again."

The theme of loneliness in old age is shown graphically by Jenkins in his poem. The speaker, the son, does not seem to look up to his parents or enjoy their company. He does not like their choice of "soaps and game shows" just as they are not drawn to his food choices, preferring "English, bland, familiar flavours." Perhaps Jenkins is also bringing attention to the generation gap that breaks down family relationships. However, the speaker in "Effects" also remembers with remorse how he did not visit his widowed mother for many weeks while she "sat night after night and stared unseeing at the television, at her inner weather," drinking whiskey and drifting towards mental health issues.

Jenkins' repetition of key words and phrases as the mother waits in the psychiatric ward for the son to visit, such as "blinked unseeing," at the wall or "blinked and stared," at nothingness, place a heavy burden of guilt on the son who left even when his mother's last words to him were "*Please don't leave.*" In the last lines, the poet describes the sadness and regret of the narrator who came too late, to hold "the blotched and crinkled hand whose fingers couldn't clasp mine anymore."

In this powerful confessional elegiac poem, Jenkins uses the title "Effects" to symbolize the little bag containing the deceased mother's belongings as well as the impact of her death on him. Would he be ever able to forget his deliberate desertion of her in her old age?

It is interesting to note that the speaker's own hand also remains in focus as the other hand that he is holding. The two hands, one living and the other motionless, show the broken ties between the mother and her son. The gesture to "clasp" his mother comes too late.

Because both poems are in first-person, the individualized voices and characters of the narrators become significant to our discussion. In a dramatic monologue, the speaker unveils their inner self through their choice of words and images. We can see that the voice in "Genetics" is joyful and optimistic and the imagery reflects that mood. Morrissey crafts a person who believes in the simple pleasures of life, someone who sees positivity in all things. The speaker is also in love which can explain her high happiness index. In contrast, the narrator in "Effects" is undergoing trauma following the demise of his mother, given that he was not there for her when she needed him. The shock of seeing her as just another body, wearing a "thick rubber band with her name on it," brings to him a rush of guilt and pain. Jenkins portrays this man as deeply introspective, and presents the structure of his monologue in the style of stream of consciousness technique. The continuous flow of the narrator's thoughts, that cannot be structured into separate stanzas, are conveyed through a single, unbroken passage. The dominant mood of "Effects" is serious and emotional, given the loss of the narrator's mother.

# Glossary

**Alliteration**: A repetition of consonants within a single line for creating stylistic effects.

**Allusion**: A reference, either explicit or indirect, to a well-known person, place, event, or another literary work.

**Ambiguity**: Use of language where more than one level of meaning or interpretation can be formed in the mind of the reader.

**Ambivalence**: A text which displays more than one attitude of the writer towards the theme, or character.

**Analogy**: A comparison that implies sameness in concept rather than similarity in appearance or qualities.

**Anaphora**: A figure of speech in which words repeat at the beginning of successive clauses, phrases, or sentences.

**Assonance**: The repetition of identical or similar vowel sounds within the same line or stanza.

**Biblical**: Relating to, or found in the Bible.

**Bildungsroman**: A German term signifying a "novel of formation" or "novel of education." It can be used to describe a character's development of mind and temperament from childhood to maturity.

**Black Humour**: A humourous way of conveying a ghastly or morbid situation.

**Blank verse:** Unrhymed poetry that is close to the natural flow of speech or prose.

**Britannia:** A personification or symbol of Britain, traditionally represented as a female warrior.

**Cacophony:** A literary device that uses harsh and jarring sounds to create dissonance in a poem.

**Centre and the Margins:** A concept that began within post-colonial and feminist discourse to identify the hierarchical divisions of social and economic power in the world. Now commonly used in literary criticism to identify the seats of power in a poem or narrative. Marginalized groups lack equal opportunities and access to the resources that are controlled by the centre. They are also generally unable to have a say in decision-making.

**Chorus:** Reference to the masked actors in ancient Greek drama who served as commentators on the main action or events. In modern dramatic usage the Chorus can represent a character or group of characters who speak directly to the audience.

**Chronological:** Following a linear order of presentation in fiction.

**Colloquial:** A conversational or non-formal speech or writing.

**Conceit:** A surprising comparison between things that do not have much in common.

**Concrete and abstract nouns:** Concrete nouns refer to material things or qualities that can be perceived by the five senses. Abstract nouns refer to words that denote immaterial attributes of persons or things such as emotions and states of mind like hope, despair.

**Context:** The social, historical conditions in which speech or writing is produced.

**Connotation:** The associations attached to a word in addition to its dictionary meaning. For example, the word "winter" would have connotations of old age, inertia, or period of decline.

**Conventions/conventional:** traditional forms and techniques that recur in literature or traditional norms of behaviour recognized by society.

**Denotation:** The exact dictionary meaning of a word. For example, the word "Spring" denotes a season following winter.

**Dialect:** A language variety used by people with a common regional or social background, usually non-standard in nature.

**Dissonance:** Language that sounds unmusical, harsh, or discordant.

**Dramatic monologue:** A type of lyric poem where a persona utters the monologue in a specific situation with the unintentional revelation of his or her own temperament or character. This type of poem normally includes an implied listener who is the primary audience.

**Elegy:** A formal and sustained lament for the death of a particular person usually written in elegiac meter (alternating hexameter and pentameter lines). In present usage, a sad or meditative poem on the theme of death or loss.

**Enjambment:** A poetic technique in which the line of verse flows into the next line without punctuation of any sort.

**Epilogue:** A piece of text that is added to the end of a play or book and which contains a conclusion.

**Euphemism:** A polite expression used instead of a harsh, taboo, or offensive phrase.

**Fall**: A biblical reference to the expulsion of Adam and Eve from the Garden of Eden.

**First-person voice**: In poetry or fiction where the narrator uses "I" or "We" to signify a subjective viewpoint.

**Foreshadowing**: A literary technique used to indicate implicitly what will happen in the story.

**Free verse**: Poetry written without any fixed form, structure, or rhythm. Derived from the French *vers libre* form.

**Fragment**: An utterance that is not a complete sentence; broken or incomplete. A poem that appears fragmented due to the disjointed arrangement of its lines.

**Graphic imagery**: Explicit, uninhibited, vivid details given in a poem, narrative, or work of art.

**Hyperbole**: The use of exaggeration in order to emphasize or create strong impressions in the audience.

**Irregular stanza**: Stanzas within a poem that have uneven lengths or different number of lines.

**Intertextuality**: When a writer makes a conscious or deliberate attempt to create interconnections with another literary text which can be perceived by a reader or audience. The way in which literary texts are shaped or influenced by another in terms of themes, ideas, or structure.

**Irony**: When the audience recognizes the difference between the surface meaning and the concealed, opposite meaning of a word or phrase. Irony is usually implied, and suggests a contrast between expectations and reality.

**Metaphysical poets**: A group of seventeenth century poets whose work is characterized by the use of logic and argument as well as witty conceits to express emotional states. Members of the group include John Donne, George Herbert, and Andrew Marvell.

**Monologue**: Speech or writing produced, and often performed by one person.

**Narrator**: The speaker or persona who narrates the events of a novel or narrative poem.

**Neologism**: A new or invented word or phrase. Also known as "coinage."

**Non-standard English**: Language that does not follow rules of standard or socially prestigious English usage. It includes the use of dialects, slang, and neologisms.

**Ode**: A lengthy verse form that is serious in nature, and generally contemplative and lyrical.

**Onomatopoeia**: A literary device that creates the sound denoted by a word or where the word itself mimics the sound. For example, *crack*, *buzz*, *splash*, etc.

**Parody**: A work that intentionally copies another work in order to ridicule it.

**Persona**: A voice chosen by the author for an artistic purpose. A persona is an invented character, not to be confused with the author or poet.

**Personification**: When human feelings or physical qualities are attributed to an inanimate object or abstract ideas.

**Poetic**: The use of language, literary devices, and meaning to create an imaginative and emotional piece of writing.

**Point of view**: The attitudes and ideas displayed by the speaker or narrator in a poem or story.

**Polyphony**: A literary feature where the text includes simultaneous, multiple voices and viewpoints.

**Prosaic**: Having the qualities of prose rather than poetry. Any kind of writing that is not poetic.

**Protagonist**: The main character or speaker in a poem, monologue, play or story.

**Realism**: Literary realism is a technique in which authors describe people and situations as they are without romanticizing them.

**Refrain**: Repetition throughout a poem of a phrase, line, or series of lines for the sake of emphasis or artistic effects.

**Renaissance**: A historical period following the Middle Ages that began in Europe in the fourteenth century and lasted until the seventeenth century. A period characterized by revival in Literature, Arts, Architecture, and other fields.

**Role reversal**: A situation in which two people change their usual roles or duties.

**Satire**: It can be described as the literary art of diminishing or ridiculing a subject by directly evoking towards it attitudes of amusement, scorn, or indignation.

**Self and the Other**: Within literary criticism and post-colonial literature, the concept refers to a group that dominates or excludes the other, less familiar. For example, the imperialists saw the colonized as the Other. It is an antithetical way of thinking about human relationships or connections.

**Semantic field:** Areas of meaning identified by a set of mutually defining words or lexemes that refer to a specific subject. For example, the group of words referring to hospitals may consist of "nurses, night duty, wards, medicines, surgery", etc.

**Slang:** Informal words or phrases used within certain social groups or age groups.

**Standard English:** The form of English used in official communication and accepted as the norm in society. Language that is less formal or differs from this standard is known as **non-standard.**

**Stream of consciousness:** A style of writing that depicts a character's thoughts and feelings as a flow rather than as a structured utterance.

**Symbolism:** Where objects or actions are given a greater significance beyond their normal qualities.

**Synecdoche:** A device in which a part is used to represent the whole.

**Taboo language:** Words or phrases that are explicit, unpleasant, and offensive.

**Title:** Please see the note below*

**Tragic drama:** A type of serious drama that flourished during ancient Greece in which sorrowful events were caused by the heroic character who suffered from a tragic flaw.

**Understatement:** A statement that describes a serious issue in a way that makes it less important.

**Utterance:** A piece of spoken language especially in a poem or a play.

**Villanelle:** A poem of nineteen lines that follows a strict form of five tercets and a concluding quatrain.

## *A Note on Titles

Writing a poem is a craft that demands deliberate word choices, and well-thought-out titles, among other factors. Sometimes a title can echo a well-known older literary text, and at other times it can be symbolic or ironical. Many times, it can simply be a straight forward descriptive word or phrase.

*Symbolic/Intertextual titles*: The connection between the literal meaning of a title and its metaphorical associations within the context of the poem is something that a poet keeps in mind while naming the piece. Sometimes a poet thinks of a past poem, a title, around which a whole new poem is constructed. Keats' Ode to a Grecian Urn was written in the Romantic period, yet this poem's title, ideas and techniques are made use of in Tim Turnbull's "Ode to a Grayson Perry Urn."

*Ironical titles*: Sometimes a poem's title means the opposite to what the poet conveys in the body of the work. "An Easy Passage," the title of a poem where two young girls come of age in a same sex relationship, presents the difficulties that these girls are not aware of. Other ironic titles come to mind – "A Minor Role," and "Song" represent the contrasting sides of human relations and social movements.

*Local colour*: Ruth Pedal's title "You, Shiva, and my Mum" evokes cultural reference that western readers may be unaware of. The poet brings in geographical specificity through her title as the poem is entirely set in India. Similarly, Daljit Nagra makes a reference to Dover, a British port in his title, "Look! I have Coming to Dover!" The poem is about immigrants arriving in Britain so the name of the port of entry becomes significant. At the same time the poet makes deliberate use of non-standard English to highlight the struggle and excitement of new immigrants.

# Bibliography

## Books

Abrams, M. H. *A Glossary of Literary Terms.* 5ᵗʰ edition, 1988.

Croft, Steven et al. *Exploring Language and Literature.* Oxford: Oxford University Press, 2001.

*Poems of the Decade: An Anthology of the Forward Books of Poetry.* Selected by William Sieghart. London: Forward Worldwide, 2011.

## Links

<https://www.theguardian.com/books/2015/mar/16/poems-of-the-decade-anthology-forward-prizes>

<https://en.wikipedia.org/wiki/Deep_image>

<https://blogasenglish.wordpress.com/2016/03/09/a-minor-role-ua-fanthorpe/>

<https://blogasenglish.wordpress.com/2016/03/03/the-lammas-hireling-revision-notes/>

<https://interpreture.com/on-her-blindness-poem-analysis/>

<https://en.wikipedia.org/wiki/Ould_Lammas_Fair>

<https://interpreture.com/you-shiva-and-my-mum-poem-analysis/>

<https://blogasenglish.wordpress.com/2016/01/13/inheritance-revision-notes/>

<https://thinkingliterature.com/seamus-heaneys-poetic-writing-style/>

<https://www.theguardian.com/books/2009/may/01/carol-ann-duffy-poet-laureate>

"Poems of the Decade anthology swaps Keats for modern masters" in *The Guardian* by Alison Flood comments on Turnbull's prize-winning poem.

# Index

Printed by
CPI books GmbH, Leck